A Rollercoaster of Literary Fun!

"Once readers orient themselves with the idiosyncrasies in Hatz's darkly whimsical—yet ultimately relatable—novel, they're in for a fast paced, entertaining comic treat. Character-driven, this loopy satire is a droll examination of the corporate-music world."

-- *Kirkus Reviews*

"*Rock Gods & Messy Monsters* by Diane Hatz is a bullet-hell critique of corporate and mass culture by way of Theodor Adorno filtered through the whimsy and humor of writers like Terry Pratchett and Kurt Vonnegut....The best kind of absurdism; the kind that wears a veneer of the surreal while having the grisly guts of reality right underneath."

-- *Independent Book Review*

"Everyone must read this book. It's exactly what I didn't know I needed – medicine for the soul and spirit disguised as a Voodoo Donut plastered in Fruity Pebbles. It reads like *SNL* meets *Wizard of Oz* meets *Matrix* meets *Succession* – and it's fantastic."

-- *E. Siboldt, filmmaker*

"A Swiftian take on the 1990s music industry viewed through a Daliesque lens, *Rock Gods & Messy Monsters* is a deft satire on corporate culture that will resonate with anyone who has ever worked in a corporate environment. A rollicking good read with memorable characters and insane -- albeit relatable -- situations…"

--*JP Gardner, Survivor of a Fortune 10 Conglomerate*

Rock Gods

&

Messy Monsters

By Diane Hatz

#rockgod #messymonster

Rock Gods & Messy Monsters
© 2022 by Diane Hatz

All rights reserved. Printed in the United States of America
Published by Whole Healthy Group LLC
Santa Fe, New Mexico

ISBN 979-8-9862823-2-9

ISBN (e-book) 979-8-9862823-1-2
Library of Congress Control Number: 2022916349

For information regarding permissions or media inquiries,
please visit www.wholehealthygroup.com or email
Rock.Gods@yahoo.com

Visit dianehatz.substack.com for an in-depth look at the symbolism
and meaning throughout the book.

To purchase additional copies, please visit
www.rockgodsandmessymonsters.com
or your preferred online bookseller.

Cover Design by Kri Pelletier, @Firehorsewest

Originally published as **Rock Gods of Acht,** © Diane Hatz 2008
ISBN 978-1-4357-1768-8

*This book is dedicated to everyone who's ever felt
put down, cast aside, or trodden upon.*

May you have the courage to find your voice and spread your wings wide.

Fly free.

And never forget -

You matter.

Preface

Rock Gods & Messy Monsters is as relevant today as when initially published in 2008, if not more so. The book is a cautionary tale that illustrates how dreams can turn into real-life nightmares. It's a #MeToo epic set in a fictional record company before the #MeToo movement.

Rock Gods & Messy Monsters is a reminder that we create our reality, and we also have the power to reinvent ourselves at any time.

I'm deeply grateful to all the women whose tenacity for the truth and perseverance under extreme duress changed the course of business over the past decade. I never believed any abusive or unethical people in positions of power would be toppled.

May you always have the strength to believe in yourself. May you always have the self-love to leave any situation holding you back. And may you always do so with grace and gratitude.

With deepest appreciation,

Diane

Diane Hatz
Santa Fe, NM
July 2022

One

The blood didn't bother Alex but cleaning it up made her angry.

"Damn it," she cursed aloud as she surveyed the red stained walls and coagulated mounds of Langley ooze around her boss' corner office.

Alex returned to her desk, her wildly improbable blonde hair already streaked stress magenta and anger black. It was coming to an end; Alex had to get out of her job. But with the worldwide recession and lines of job applicants she saw every day on her way into the building, she was lucky to have a job, especially in a major record company.

Alex put her backpack on the floor and unzipped the side of her head. She reached in and pulled out her brain, placing the throbbing gray matter in the customized, faux crystal cerebrum urn Acht Records had supplied her with her first day at the company. She had fought the procedure at first, refused to sign the Cerebrum Extraction Release form, but with times being as hard as they were, and with the knowledge that she had spent over six months unemployed before being offered this job, Alex knew she had no choice.

And after wandering through the homogenous maze of Acht, up and down forty floors of identical gray hallways and glaring fluorescent lights, she had realized she would be better off if she removed all traces of thought and intelligence before commencing employment at the company. Unfortunately, these days she seemed to be developing the ability to think and feel without a brain in her head. And that couldn't be good.

Dread and negativity washed over her. Langley was nearing. She looked up and smiled brainlessly as her five foot six, blood encrusted boss stormed past her and into his office.

"ALEX!" blew out of Langley's door and into Alex's face.

She leapt to attention, her body automatically responding to the tone of his voice, and quickly entered his domain.

Langley glared at her, his short Germanic blonde hair standing straight on end while his standard two cigarettes were both lit and smoking in his battery-operated smokeless ashtray. His brown eyes bulged from their sockets, a precursor to a childish tantrum and possible blood vessel explosion.

Langley pointed to the ooze-stained walls of his corporate executive office, his hand shaking with uncontrollable rage. "Why isn't this mess clean?!"

Alex rushed to the oak cabinet end table next to Langley's brown, calf skin sofa. She opened the door and snapped on her Playtex rubber gloves. She grabbed the sponge and ever-waiting bucket filled with sudsy water and attacked the walls with the vengeance of a professional cleaning woman. She wiped; she washed; she dunked and wrung. Her arms moved with lightning speed as she attempted to return the walls to their original executive office ivory, regulation color.

When the water turned the same deep red as the coagulated floret of blood dangling precariously from Langley's neck, she knew she had to regroup and prepare herself for the second round of cleaning. Alex hurried out of Langley's office, the bucket of now-sudsy blood firmly in her grasp yet still sloshing about her. She rushed into the corporate executive supply closet laundry room and emptied the blood water into the industrial-sized sink installed for just such emergencies. She rinsed the sponge as best she could and refilled the bucket with wall cleaner and water.

She returned to Langley's office and washed once again, trying to remove the magenta hue. When the walls diminished to a light pink tone, Alex realized she could clean no better, so she returned her cleaning equipment to its proper place and returned to her desk.

She sat uncomfortably in her Acht-issued black vinyl chair and fidgeted with the back-support cushion she had to buy after her ergonomically correct, company regulation seat nearly landed her in the hospital with back trauma. The company doctor blamed it on lack of exercise, not on the soft, unsupported, low-back chairs all the secretaries were forced to sit in. Alex turned on her computer and squinted through the glare from the overhead fluorescent lights. She typed in Langley's revisions to his daily itinerary, reverse alphabetizing the executives who were also joining President DiMachio for lunch at one o'clock.

The shock brought her to her feet. Langley had embedded neurological electric shock chips in Alex's body when she first started working for him, so with the push of a button, he could get her attention anywhere in the building. The second jolt ripped through Alex's ankles and nearly toppled her. If she didn't carry out her duty quickly, he would start shocking her all over.

Alex hobbled around her desk and out of her secretarial suite, limping down the hall toward the vending area and executive kitchen. As she turned the corner, she glanced through the doorway of the neighboring executive office and saw the Senior Vice President of Promotion's lingerie-exposed secretary sitting contentedly behind her desk, busily preparing herself for another day of doing nothing.

Doing nothing can be a difficult achievement, especially when there was work to do, but Zena excelled. Her brain floated happily through clear cerebrum nutrient juice in the synthetic crystal Acht urn she proudly displayed on her desk. Zena was so proud to display her brain to any passerby she often left what she called her inner self in the urn full time, even at night and on weekends. Sometimes the promotion secretary would even sneak the vessel out of the building, her brain still swimming in nutrient juice, so she could show herself off to friends and family.

When Alex limped past Hellie, the executive helmsman and senior level receptionist, she knew she was nearing her intended destination. Alex had no time to stop and exchange their usual morning hello, but Hellie herself seemed preoccupied as she faced the aquarium stationed on her desk and tapped a light melodic tune on the fish tank glass with her regulation Ticonderoga number two pencil. Inside, twelve mutant sea creatures swam through the water, their tails swishing in time to the beat.

As Alex approached the vending area, she saw movement out of the corner of her eye. It was a brief flash, a whirlwind of repressed energy, but she thought she saw a tall, gangly man zipping down the hallway, handing cassettes to people right and left. She turned her head and saw him, head to toe in blue, even his hair and skin. When he whizzed by the snack area, emitting a short, dry cough, he tossed a cassette in Alex's direction. She caught the tape and looked down at the blue casing, noticing the band's name was "Bleu". By the time she looked up, he had disappeared around the corner, remaining only a vague memory and a flash of color.

"The Roadrunner," said Alex as she stared into the emptiness left in the man's wake.

The executive secretary stepped into the snack machine alcove. Langley insisted on a cup of black coffee and a packet of Twinkies every morning, though Alex never quite understood what he did with the twin golden sponge cakes. Every day between eleven and two o'clock, not long after Langley would arrive at work, Alex would enter his executive domain and find crumbs and splotches of white cream scattered about his desk and office. It seemed that more Twinkie fell about the room than into Langley's mouth.

Alex pressed her face against the glass of all four machines, searching behind the bags and bars of chips, crackers and candy, hoping a packet of the golden sponge cakes had accidentally strayed into another row of junk food. She cringed when she realized the Twinkies were gone. Alex filled a special-ordered Styrofoam cup with steaming black coffee and sighed from an emptiness that overwhelmed her from within.

She pulled out two dollars from the emergency snack fund she had recently begun keeping in her pockets and put them into the vending machine. She pressed the appropriate buttons and pulled out a packet of nacho cheese Doritos and a bag of Whoppers malted milk balls. She returned to her desk, her hands clutching her snacks and her boss' coffee while her hair flew wild and stress magenta behind her, a flag to her every mood and feeling.

Alex breathlessly entered Langley's office and placed the cup of coffee on his desk. She rarely looked at him, but when she saw his arm reach out for the cup, and noticed even it was purple with rage, she stepped back and trembled.

Today was not going to be a good day.

Two

Vinny DiMachio turned on his private television surveillance monitor and leaned back in his fur lined gilt trimmed leather throne, a grin slowly sliming its way across his pockmarked, reptilian face. He enjoyed this part of his staff lunches the most, the time when he could secretly observe his executive staff as they gathered in the executive boardroom one floor above him, anxiously awaiting his arrival and not knowing DiMachio could see and hear their every move.

The cameras were mandatory ever since the death threats in the mid-eighties. The guilty party was never found, but rumors ran rampant that the person issuing the threats was a member of his executive staff, so DiMachio had surveillance cameras installed in the corporate executive boardroom, as well as the executive elevators and bathrooms, to discreetly observe his staff for any signs of disloyalty or possible mutiny. He was even considering bugging devices in the executives' offices.

He couldn't be too careful; after all, he was President and Ruling Dictator of Acht Records, as well as President of the Domestic Division, President of International, CEO, COO, CFO, Chairman, Czar, and any other combination of letters that made him look important. He had fought for twenty years to get to his current position, and many people had been used as steppingstones and fall guys for his twisted yet always upward moving career path. DiMachio's vision and driving motivational force behind every move he made was his obsession to become the wealthiest and most powerful person in the music business, at any cost. And with those aspirations, tight security was essential to monitor his wellbeing and keep an eye on any matters of interest.

Next to DiMachio, resting comfortably yet slowly stiffening with interest and anticipation, sat Jeremy Wickett, DiMachio's most faithful and trusted ally and confidante. DiMachio and Jeremy Wickett had known each other from birth, and each year brought them closer and closer. And because of that inseparable bond, that underlying trust of a blood brother, DiMachio made sure Jeremy was by his side, as an aide or a vice to whatever position DiMachio was in. Jeremy deservedly held the titles of Executive Vice President of the Domestic Division, Executive Vice President of International, Executive Vice CEO, Executive Vice COO, Executive Vice CFO, Executive Vice Chairman, Executive Vice Czar, and Executive Vice of everything else DiMachio decided he wanted to be.

DiMachio and Jeremy rested comfortably in their throne, surrounded by the countless gold and platinum records that hung from the walls of their football-field-sized office, an office that took up the entire thirty sixth floor. DiMachio routinely called executive meetings; he liked keeping his staff alert and on their toes, and he especially enjoyed their company when he conveniently forgot to mention the topic for discussion.

"It's showtime," said DiMachio as Jiglio entered the boardroom, his blue pinstripe polyester suit as creaseless as a sheet of newly formed ice. Jiglio casually wandered around the massive, handmade mahogany boardroom table and across the plush, blood red carpet toward one of only two standard-sized windows in the corporate monolith recently renamed Acht. He strolled past the priceless oil paintings on the dark, mahogany walls, not even glancing at the Pollock DiMachio's financial consultant advised would be a good tax write off, and looked through the glass at the city before him.

"I don't know, Jeremy," said DiMachio as he pushed a button and one of the cameras zoomed in on Jiglio's face. "Something's different. Nothing serious, but something doesn't seem right."

DiMachio and Jeremy studied Jiglio's face for any telltale signs of underhandedness or disloyalty, but the Senior Vice President of Promotion appeared ice calm and as corporately disinterested as ever.

"He looks the same," said DiMachio as he scrutinized the two festering boils on the Senior Vice President's forehead. He continued looking for several more seconds but couldn't see anything different. "Maybe he's just up to his usual underhanded promotion schemes."

DiMachio dismissed Jiglio as Weena, the Senior Vice President of Media Relations, rolled her two hundred pound plus, five-foot, two-inch frame through the conference room door.

"Oh, my," was the only noise to escape as Weena found herself face to face with Jiglio.

"Do it," said DiMachio as he leaned closer to the screen and watched his two executives.

In a nervous frenzy, Weena waddled around the thirty-foot long conference room table and deposited herself in a chair as far away from Jiglio as corporately acceptable. Jiglio sat six seats away on the other side of the table, his steely black eyes locking on to Weena.

They all heard the soft thud as Weena's right ear fell limply on the table. She nervously pulled out the economy size tube of Medical Repair and Reattachment Glue she carried everywhere in the Acht medical bag repair kit the company had supplied her with once the company doctor realized she tended to lose body parts. He had wanted to surgically implant the kit in her hip, but Weena had resisted, promising to carry it in her black canvas shoulder bag briefcase. Weena retrieved the severed body part and unscrewed the tube of glue, expertly dampening the rim of her ear and making sure to use just enough repair ointment for proper adhesion, yet not too much to cause messy glue leakage.

Weena raised her ear toward her head. As her hand reached shoulder level, she accidentally locked eyes with Jiglio. She gasped and involuntarily jumped with fright. They watched in slow motion helplessness as her body part soared upward and then began its downward descent toward the conference room table.

Her ear landed glue-side down with an air of finality, the Medical Repair and Reattachment ointment immediately affixing her body part to the table. Weena grabbed her appendage in horror and desperately tried to peel it off the varnished wood; her fingers rolled, picked and plucked, stretching her ear and nearly tearing it, but the repair glue lived up to its advertising claims and bonded instantly.

DiMachio watched as Jiglio reached into his pocket, pulled out his Swiss army knife, and slid it across the boardroom table. The mere sight of an object owned by Jiglio was enough to make Weena lose three fingers. She clumsily opened the knife with what few fingers she had left and began slicing through the glue. Her attempts were futile, once the glue adhered it was permanent, so she had no choice but to slice through her ear, leaving behind a thin layer of glued flesh. Weena picked up what was left of her body part, collected her missing fingers, and turned her back to Jiglio.

"Pathetic," was all DiMachio said as he watched Weena put herself back together.

"Hosannah," he bellowed to one of his assistants through his speakerphone intercom. "When lunch is over, get maintenance to the boardroom with sandpaper. Tell 'em to remove the flesh from the table." He paused, then added, "And make sure there isn't a scratch. I'll be checking."

"Yes, Mr. DiMachio."

"Damn it," he said to his faithful aide and sidekick, Jeremy Wickett, as he turned back to the television screen. "Only four body parts." A dissatisfied grunt escaped his lips as he watched Weena reattach the last of her body parts. "Jiglio's got a long way if he expects ten body parts in ten minutes by the end of the year."

Senior Vice President of Sales and Marketing Derby entered the conference room, his ornate silver fork nestled comfortably behind his greasy, sweaty ear. He walked around the table, his overstuffed, basketball-sized belly full of airline food, hotel mini bar treats, and junk food snack fat leading the way. Derby sat two seats away from Weena, brushing his one strand of greasy hair across his almost bald head.

As Derby rebuttoned the two buttons that had popped open at the bulging stomach of his pastel pink, polyester rayon mix shirt, the door flew open of its own accord. A gale force wind swept through the room, announcing the arrival of the tantrum prone and highly explosive Senior Vice President of Business Affairs and Law, and General Counsel, Langley. He stormed into the room, his arms and face strangulated purple, a lit cigarette dangling precariously from his mouth while smoke curled around his nostrils and ears. He walked around the table and sat in his unofficially official seat away from the others, his banishment from the intimacy of their company due to both the cigarette stench that permanently followed him and his tendency to explode and splatter blood over anyone unfortunate enough to be nearby.

His eyes darted back and forth, and his legs bounced uncontrollably from the five cups of morning coffee delivered one after the other by his electronically monitored assistant, Alex. He whipped his portable smokeless ashtray out of his pocket and caught the one-inch ash that had just fallen from his cigarette and was heading toward DiMachio's priceless conference room table. Langley placed the ashtray down and rested his cigarette in it. As soon as the first cigarette was out of Langley's hands, he immediately lit a second.

Smoke danced throughout the room, slowly spreading its fingers to all corners of the meeting area. Weena coughed and waved her digit restored hand through the air, trying to fan away the growing stench. She reached into her black canvas shoulder bag briefcase and pulled out a miniature, battery operated fan, placing it on the table. She turned the power on high and pointed the battery generated waft of air in Langley's direction.

"Heysannah, better ventilation system in the boardroom."

"Yes, Mr. DiMachio."

DiMachio glanced at his watch. Two minutes before one. He turned his attention back to the surveillance monitor and watched as each of the Senior Vice Presidents occupied themselves. Jiglio read *Billboard* magazine, undoubtedly searching for photos of himself in the weekly music trade publication. Weena thumbed through the calendar in her Filofax, her eyes most likely skimming the blank evenings and unmarked weekends of her life, dates only ever filled with work related events. Derby had pulled a miscellaneous food product out of his pocket and was preoccupied with chewing and spilling crumbs down his shirt and onto the table. Langley was settled at the far end of the table, lighting cigarettes, taking a few drags, then absentmindedly leaving them burning in the ashtray as he lit up another.

The silence was broken as the Senior Vice President of Artists and Repertoire, or A&R, casually opened the door and sauntered into the room, his music player headphones surgically implanted in his ears.

"Hey, everyone," said Skeater through music blaring only in his head.

He bobbed to the beat and waved his right arm in a friendly greeting. His left arm cuddled a mounted stuffed ferret, his once living pet Skat. The other senior vice presidents looked briefly at him, some with disdain, some with indifference, but none acknowledging his greeting. Each executive turned back to whatever distraction had been saving them from casual conversation, something none of them excelled at.

"Hosannah, we're ready," said DiMachio after each of his executives had glanced at their watch at least once. He and Jeremy knew the later they arrived, the more hectic and important they appeared, thus creating the aura of that much more power and status. And there was an unwritten rule in business that the higher people rose in a corporation, the later they could arrive in meetings.

Hosannah, the Swedish twin assistant, the Doublemint Girl of Rock, entered the President's office and sat behind the wheel of the Acht presidential transmobile. She drove the electric golf cart type vehicle over to DiMachio's desk. Once the President and his aide were comfortably settled in the back seat, they were slowly driven across his football-field-sized office toward the presidential elevator.

DiMachio and Jeremy were dropped off at the door of the executive boardroom. They entered without a word.

"Listen," said Jiglio as he came to life and laid his music industry magazine on the table. He placed his finger on the opened page and moved it across the lines as he read. "Despite rumors to the contrary, Acht Records, formerly USA Records, has reported increased profits and revenues for the second quarter of the fiscal year. Even industry insiders were surprised at the success the company is having so soon after a major buy out and a mediocre previous year."

"Bravo. Of course. We knew it would happen," echoed around the room.

Weena leaned forward, her eyes aglow. "Press releases are out everywhere, every trade magazine, every video channel, every outlet even remotely interested in music and the music business. We're letting the world know Acht is number one."

"Always getting press, always doing a great job," said Derby.

"Why, thank you, Derby." A slight blush appeared on Weena's cheeks.

"Everyone's been working hard, doing a good job," said Langley. "We should all congratulate ourselves."

"Yes, yes, certainly," echoed around the table.

DiMachio and Jeremy took their seat in the jewel studded throne at the head of the table as invisible waiters silently began serving lunch. Plates of veal piccata, served over fresh linguine and surrounded by buttered asparagus, floated through the air and were served to most of

10

the executives. Skeater nodded his thanks to the empty space next to him as an all-natural veggie burger, French fries, and garden salad were set down before him, accompanied by a silver condiment tray filled with dishes of ketchup, mustard, relish, onions, and horseradish.

DiMachio sensed the apprehension surrounding his vice presidents, all except Skeater hungrily spooning ketchup onto his fries. DiMachio watched as Langley pulled out what looked like a pocket-sized calculator and pounded several buttons. The executives never quite recovered from the last great reorganization in 1990, and DiMachio knew they were nervous that the recent minor changes and firing of lower-level managers and directors would eventually impact them.

When the wine and water glasses were filled, and objects stopped floating through the room, President and Ruling Dictator DiMachio looked at each executive until he had their full attention. DiMachio raised his wine glass as he did before every executive luncheon.

"Glad you could make it."

Jiglio, Weena, Derby and Langley raised their glasses and returned the obligatory toast.

"Glad to be here."

"Cheers," said Skeater as he raised his glass of iced herbal raspberry tea.

DiMachio sipped the vintage Bordeaux and slipped into his friendly corporate facade. "I guess you're wondering why I called you for lunch." He paused briefly, then let out a small, synthetic chuckle as he looked over his executive staff. "Though we know it's partly because I enjoy your company so much."

"Here, here," his executives replied, their smiles equally as plastic.

The heavy oak boardroom doors silently swung open. DiMachio glanced up and saw a woman with wildly improbable magenta streaked blonde hair limp into the room, a carton of Winstons under her arm. She made her way over to Senior Vice President of Business Affairs and Law, and General Counsel, Langley, and placed the cigarettes in front of him. He ripped open the carton and pulled out a pack. He thrust the rest of the carton back into the woman's hands and quietly hissed, "One, I punched in one."

The woman's hair became more magenta as her face hardened. She disappeared from the room, limping away with the now opened carton of cigarettes as quietly as she had arrived.

DiMachio picked up his knife and fork and attacked his meat, shredding the baby calf to pieces before placing anything into his mouth. He had met with his executives six months earlier on the day the takeover was officially announced, but he had been no more than vaguely positive, and he gave no clues or details as to what the future would hold. He had planned it that way.

When DiMachio had leisurely finished his last bite of veal and wiped his mouth with the cloth napkin that had been placed on his lap, he spoke. "I summoned you to discuss the takeover by the Yakadans."

DiMachio felt the hardening in Jeremy Wickett as the anxiety level rose in the room. Langley had three Winston's lit at the same time and was alternating between them, sometimes puffing off two at once while trying to eat his meal. Weena's nose fell into the slaughtered calf meat and became lost in the linguine. Inexplicably, the Medical Repair and Reattachment Glue that Weena used, that bonded any two materials known to mankind together, became ineffective when she endured severe stress. All types of bonding agents had been tested, but Weena's body chemistry and stress sweat found a way to deactivate the bonding agents in the glue, making the permanent only temporary, the glued unglued.

DiMachio waited until she found her body part, wiped it clean and reglued it to her face. He continued. "We all know the Yakadans bought USA Records almost a year ago and renamed the company Acht. As of today, the change is official. A memo is being circulated to employees as we speak. All references to USA, all leftover letterhead, memo paper, envelopes, business cards, everything, must be destroyed immediately. The transition has been finalized; USA Records is no more."

DiMachio would never admit it publicly, but he was sad to see USA Records gone from the music industry map. He had given twenty years of his life to the company, had risen through the ranks and fought his way to the top of the ladder, all through his own ingenuity and with the help of only one confidante and ally, Jeremy Wickett.

He had wild times; his drug years were spent touring with the popular bands of the late sixties and seventies, supplying and sharing drugs and alcohol with the musicians on the label, and having every type and kind of sex imaginable.

DiMachio sighed. Those were the days. But when he hit his mid-thirties and was forced to decide between early career death burnout or old age retirement survival, he signed himself into a detox clinic, along with hundreds of his peers, and learned to face his future drug and almost alcohol free. No one could ever deny him a good glass of wine.

But with those vices gone, he had turned his attention to the ego addiction of power. It was almost the same high as drugs, and, for the most part, legal. Hand in hand with power was money, so when the Yakadans bought out USA Records and asked DiMachio to continue as president, with a new contract and perks the USA Board would never have thought to offer him, along with a pay raise that would bring his annual income to over ten million dollars, DiMachio knew the buyout would benefit both him and Jeremy Wickett.

"So," said DiMachio as he reached for his glass of wine. "Any questions?"

Weena's face was ashen. She took a deep breath and cleared her throat. "We've heard a lot about the Yakadans, but what's going on?" She threw up her hands for emphasis, and they stayed attached. "And where are they? I've never seen one. Rumor has it they don't exist; they say the USA Board of Directors wanted to shake things up at the company and made up the buyout in order to fire hundreds of people."

DiMachio glanced at Jeremy. Maybe someone had found out he unjustifiably engineered the Great Reorganization and Corporate Shuffling of 1990. The shakeup had not been done out of corporate necessity or reduced company profits; it was done because DiMachio knew he could validate a companywide firing and reorganization by using that year's recession as his excuse, thus eliminating anyone DiMachio didn't like or want around.

No, they couldn't have found out. He had been overly careful, overly secretive; no one except Jeremy knew what he had done.

"The Yakadans are real," said DiMachio. "They're from a galaxy outside the Milky Way, who knows where. They're evolved, very adaptable; they look like us for the most part. They want to test some kind of new technology of theirs."

"But who are these people? Where are they in the company?" asked Weena, her confidence increasing proportionally with the number of Xanax she swallowed.

DiMachio picked at his asparagus with disinterest. "You probably have. They look like us except their skin is a light shade of green, something to do with chlorophyll. Earth has become a major tourist spot, so don't be surprised if you start seeing them everywhere."

"Are they trying to take over?" asked Jiglio, his food barely touched.

DiMachio picked up the asparagus and sniffed it. Grimacing, he dropped it back onto his plate. "Not according to them. They probably want to be an economic threat, to start trading with Earth, and unless we get equal trade agreements, which don't happen often in this country, one day we might be overrun with whatever it is they make and sell." DiMachio sipped his wine. "That's not our concern. They're here, and they own the record company, but they have no intention of interfering with our day-to-day operation, so we can carry on, business as usual."

"Are any of them in the building?" asked Derby, his ornate silver fork nestled back behind his ear, waiting for dessert.

"Yes," said DiMachio. "The top three floors are for the Yakadans. They oversee from above and do whatever it is they do."

Langley stubbed out his cigarettes and concentrated on finishing his lunch.

"Jiglio, you want that?" asked Derby as he pointed toward Jiglio's nearly full plate.

"No."

Jiglio slid his food toward the Senior Vice President of Sales and Marketing Derby, as he did most staff lunches.

Derby happily retrieved his grease and sweat covered fork from behind his ear and shoveled Jiglio's lunch into his mouth, his teeth clanking noisily against his fork, his saliva working overtime as his body tried to digest the overabundance of food.

The conversation and mood remained light until everyone had finished eating and the table had been cleared by the ever attentive, yet totally invisible, waiters. When coffee and an assortment of fresh fruit and handmade Italian pastries had been served all around, and DiMachio had leisurely lit a cigar, he knew he could no longer hold out.

"Well, team," he said. "We've been through a lot with the takeover, especially the unfortunate job we had dismissing some staff over the past few months. And even though this is part of our job as senior executives, it's never fun." DiMachio and Jeremy were in their glory, feeding off the insecurities and anxieties of each person around the table. DiMachio puffed on his cigar and blew a few smoke rings. He continued. "I've been thinking the whole ordeal over. I think we've been through a lot, more stress than any executive should have to endure, so I spoke with the Yakadans and we've come up with a solution."

No one dared to breathe.

DiMachio's face cracked into one of his executive reptilian smiles as he looked over his flock. "I've decided we need to reward ourselves and the company. We deserve it."

Months of tension and anxiety exhaled simultaneously in a gust of relief. Jeremy was the only one who felt deflated, and he fell limp against his master.

DiMachio sucked on his cigar and continued. "The Yakadans don't care what we do. They're worried artists and fans might resent the takeover, and it might affect whatever they're trying to do. They want Acht Records to be an artist/people company, which means we can give ourselves and the artists whatever we want if we stay within the company budget. And the company budget is nearly twice what it was when we were USA Records."

A smile found its way on to everyone's face, even Skeater's, though he smiled reflexively through the music he had snuck back on.

"What should we do?" As soon as he asked the question, DiMachio heard nuts and bolts rattling in everyone's head as thoughts began to grind and spin out of control.

"I think we senior executives need at least twenty-five percent raises," said Langley, his veins pulsating with excitement, his pack of cigarettes nearly crumpled with joy. "If we're capped on overall salary amounts, I say freeze support staff wages. No one cares about them."

All heads nodded in agreement. DiMachio looked at Jeremy. He sensed his Executive Vice President's approval and said, "I think you have something there. Twenty-five percent is fair to me. What about the rest of you?"

Executive heads bobbed fervently.

"Fine," said DiMachio, evil shining on his pineapple pockmarked reptilian face. "Consider it done. Anything else?"

Jiglio looked at DiMachio. "We need promotions. Better titles. We've held the same position for over a year. I think it's time we stepped up a rung."

Heads once again nodded in agreement.

"Okay," said DiMachio. "Any suggestions for new titles?"

Jiglio smoothed back his dyed black hair and eyed DiMachio. "How about Senior Executive Vice President?"

Weena forgot Langley's cigarette smoke and turned the portable fan on herself, drying the sweaty beads of excitement that clung to her upper lip and forehead. "It's too much like what we have now. I think we should be Senior Senior Vice President."

"No," said Langley, his hand instinctively reaching for a cigarette. "Senior Executive Vice President sounds good to me."

Derby put down his silver fork and swallowed the remaining crumbs of lunch that had found their way into his mouth. "It's close, but it doesn't sound right yet. We're more than that."

DiMachio watched as his senior executives contemplated the new tag that would soon characterize their identity in the professional world. The music business was a matter of who you knew, who you blew, and who you screwed (over) to get to the top. A job title was a key that allowed entry behind specific locked doors, each door leading to different career paths and different status levels. Choose the wrong title and an employee could be typecast into one specific type of job and sometimes never emerge. DiMachio had no problem with his people opening new doors if they knew their place when it came to dealing with him.

A smile crept across Jiglio's stone cold face, a smile that momentarily broke the ice.

"How about this?" asked Jiglio. "Instead of being President, we promote DiMachio to Deity and Ruling Dictator. Jeremy would naturally be Executive Vice Deity and Ruling Dictator. Then we'll become Senior Senior Executive Presidents."

Langley, Weena, Derby and Jiglio looked at each other for several seconds as the sound of the proposed title sunk in. A collective smile spread around the table from one person to the next, again infecting Skeater hidden behind his wall of music.

Weena pulled on Skeater's ear lobe, turning off his music.

"Hey!"

"We just got ourselves new titles."

"Great," said Skeater.

"And raises," added Derby.

"What about the artists? Anything for them?" asked Skeater.

The table looked at him in silent disgust. Weena reached over and pulled on his ear again, turning his music back on.

DiMachio smiled, knowing instinctively that this was the job title his executives were searching for, the title that would make them stand just a little prouder while their subordinates cowered just a little lower. He felt Jeremy grow hard and stand more erect, so he congratulated his trusted confidante and closest ally with a firm pat on the back. They clung to each other and crooned with delight over their latest promotion. The ex-Senior Vice Presidents, now Senior Senior Executive Presidents, took their cue and silently slid back their chairs and exited the room, dragging Skeater and Skat with them. DiMachio was left to celebrate with his dear, dear, dear friend, Jeremy Wickett.

And so it came to pass at Acht Records that the executives were rewarded for being executives, and for no other reason, while the rest of the company carried on, their noses to the grindstone, their raises and rewards being slowly siphoned off as the senior level fattened their wallets and egos.

Three

Langley's disappearance into DiMachio's executive staff lunch meant Alex would have an unrestrained hour or two where she was free to work and carry out her responsibilities at her own pace. When she knew her boss was past the point of sudden office return, and she had ordered a case of Twinkies for future office emergencies, she wandered out to Hellie's desk, her blonde hair flowing in relaxed freedom.

As she opened her mouth to speak, the elevator bell rang. Alex turned and saw Skeater step off the car, his head bobbing while he snapped his fingers. The Senior Vice President of A&R, soon to become a Senior Senior Executive President, half walked, half jigged with his stuffed ferret Skat toward Alex and Hellie. Alex stared at the A&R man.

"Hey," said Skeater to both assistants as he tugged his right earlobe. "Where's this lunch? It's here, right?"

Alex blushed.

"It's in the boardroom on thirty-seven," said Hellie.

"Oh, wow." Skeater pulled on his ear. "Thanks," he said loudly as he turned and disappeared into an elevator.

"Alex," the receptionist said to her fellow secretary when Skeater and his ferret had disappeared. "You've got purple streaks in your hair. What's that mean?"

Alex turned to the receptionist, her face still flushed. "I don't know," she said. "But it's awfully hot in here."

Hellie turned back to her aquarium and tapped her Ticonderoga number two pencil against the fish tank glass in determined concentration. Her mutant sea creatures responded in kind by swishing their tails and swimming through the water with what was becoming synchronized grace.

"They're really coming along," said Alex as she stepped around the reception desk to get a closer look at Hellie's training methods.

"Hmmmm."

Hellie had begun her employment at Acht no more than a month earlier, a bright, cheery waif of a woman, and no more than twenty-two. During her first week at the company, the mutant sea creatures appeared in the empty terrarium fish tank that had belonged to the receptionist before her. Hellie thought the harmless sea dwellers would help her adjust to her new position, and her fellow employees welcomed her fish as they had welcomed her. No one noticed.

Alex forgot about Skeater and her horrible day as she watched Hellie tap on the glass, gently coaxing her creatures into dancing as she instructed. Hellie told Alex she had adopted the mutant sea creatures after they had literally attached themselves to her in the Hudson River. Hellie had been out on her usual kayaking trek one morning and was gliding down the waterway when she noticed something on the end of her paddle. She brought the tip in for a closer look and saw a four-inch fishlike creature attached to the piece of wood. She wasn't sure what it was; it resembled a sea horse but was purple and had small suction cups on both sides like the underside of a starfish. Two lobster-like antennae extended from either side of its head. The creature also had the same ability to survive out of water for extended amounts of time, like a crab.

Hellie was more curious than fearful about the mutant sea dweller, so she reached over and touched it. The creature turned and gazed at her with big, sad, longing eyes, and Hellie fell in love. She stroked the animal and spoke soothingly until it detached itself from the paddle and nestled in the palm of Hellie's hand, its tentacles happily stroking her skin, its suction cups massaging her flesh. When Hellie got back to the dock, she noticed eleven more sea creatures with different colors attached to the side of her kayak, so she adopted them all and gave them a home.

Hellie was curious as to what species of fish these creatures were, so she went to marine biologists, scientists, librarians, even *Ripley's Believe It or Not* to find out more about them, but no one had encountered such mutants before. The only consensus among the scientists and marine biologists was that the sea dwellers, or their parents, had most likely been exposed to the nitrates and chemical pesticides reported never to run off farmland and into the nation's water system.

The explanation seemed probable to Hellie, and even Alex had to agree it made sense, especially after witnessing their survival in Acht tap water and their appetite for moldy cheese and decayed bugs. Recently, they had also taken a liking to the white cream centers of Langley's destroyed or leftover Twinkies.

"Hi guys, what are you doing?"

Alex turned and saw Zena sauntering up to the reception area, her floral minidress swishing seductively, her front buttons undone to show off her Victoria's Secret red satin slip.

"Hellie's training her pets to dance underwater," said Alex.

"Oh," replied Zena vacantly. "Can I ask you two a question?"

"Sure," said Alex.

"Well," said Zena, a hint of shyness, a touch of naive innocence in her voice. "I was reading this magazine and I'm confused. Is Canada in the United States?"

"Excuse me?" said Alex, sure she had heard her wrong.

Zena smiled her nonthreatening, girlish smile, the kind of smile that brought out the dominant and protective traits in men. "Is Canada in the United States?"

"Are you serious?"

"Well, yeah. You know, is it a state and where exactly is it?"

Even Alex's hair was stunned. With or without a brain, Zena's lack of mental capabilities was frustrating at times. Did she act ignorant to get attention or did she really have the IQ of a pea? "Canada is another country, Zena. It's right above the U.S. Don't you ever look at a map?"

Zena lowered her eyes and put on her pity-and-love-me-for-not-being-as-smart-as-you face.

Hellie turned away from her aquarium and dance practice to stare at Zena. "It's attached to the United States, though," said Hellie helpfully. "It's the same land mass and they're both part of North America, but they're separate countries."

"Oh." Zena stared blankly at the wall for several seconds, then smiled one of her sweet sugar cookie smiles. "Thanks," she said to both

Alex and Hellie. She turned on her heel and slowly sauntered back to her secretarial suite.

Alex looked at Hellie and shook her head.

Hellie shrugged her shoulders and returned to her aquarium dance troupe.

Alex yelped as the shock ripped through her right arm. "I don't have any memos to deliver, you moron." The shock to her stomach made her double over. "His highness needs cigarettes," she said as she clutched her waist.

"Is there anything I can do?" asked Hellie.

"No, Langley does this all the time." The shock to Alex's leg nearly crippled her. "Damn him. He doesn't know which button to push, and the controls are on high." She limped back to her desk, pulled out a carton of Winstons and obediently went up to the thirty seventh floor. Interrupting executive meetings was torture, a humiliating reminder that she was in a separate class from the management level employees. Alex took a deep breath, gritted her teeth, and pushed on the heavy oak doors.

The smell of veal filled her nostrils as she limped into the room. She lowered her eyes as soon as she spotted Langley. Alex felt the silent, unwelcoming tension increase with every step as she made her way around the table toward her boss. She realized the room had frozen, not even the ice in the water glasses stirred. She was an intruder, unwanted in the executive domain only privy to the elite. She placed the carton of cigarettes on the table next to Langley's lunch. He reached out and grabbed the carton, ripping it open. He removed a pack of cigarettes and thrust the carton back toward her face.

"One, I punched in one," Langley hissed in Alex's general direction.

Wordlessly, Alex took the open carton, her face hardening with inexpressible anger.

She limped out of the room as silently as she had come, nearly crushing the cigarettes she gripped tightly in her hands.

When she returned to her floor, Hellie looked up. "Did he want cigarettes?"

Alex held up the ripped open carton. "He wanted a pack, not a carton. And he was angry I didn't know what he wanted."

Alex hobbled back to her secretarial suite and opened a packet of the emergency Twinkie supply that had just arrived via interoffice deli delivery. As she bit into the first golden sponge cake, she glanced at her watch. One thirty.

"Damn," she said as Twinkie cake spilled out of her mouth. "Personnel."

Alex stood and quickly unzipped the side of her head. She took the lid off her cerebrum urn and thrust her hands into the nutrient juice. She pulled out her brain, juice dripping over her desk and onto the floor, and shoved it into her skull, making sure to tuck in all gray matter. A week earlier Alex had been in a rush to leave work and had absentmindedly shoved her brain in and zipped herself up, not realizing part of her tissue was still hanging out. She was now extremely careful when opening and closing her head.

Alex rushed to personnel, her heart pounding, her mind racing. She walked into the reception area, her hair a deepened shade of stress magenta and sprinkled with apprehensive orange, and sat down on one of the hard, uncomfortable metal benches, adrenaline coursing through her veins. Alex hated personnel, or "human resources" as the company handbook called it. Ever since senior management decided there was no need for human representatives in personnel, she and the rest of the low level, nonexempt employees had been forced to deal with computer interface counselors, thus eliminating the human in human resources.

Alex breathed in the antiseptic smelling air and looked around the cold, sterile room as she waited for her name to appear on the digital display screen hanging on the far wall. There were three other secretaries seated near her, their vacant smiles and hollow eyes proof they had chosen to leave their brains behind. Interviewing with brains was optional at Acht.

The room itself was windowless and lit by regulation glaring white fluorescent lights. Decor consisted of several rows of metal benches facing the display screen that acted as a receptionist, with a few plastic trees dotted around for warmth. The gray walls were decorated with framed posters of the most famous acts to record for USA/Acht Records, including The Bucking D's, Ree Armstrong, Bobby Vent, and Splotch.

By the time Alex's name appeared on the digital display screen, her brain had slowed to an unstimulated, mentally catatonic state, and her adrenalin had ceased to flow. She stood up and walked to the personnel door, her backside numb from the hard bench. She typed her social security number into the keypad next to the door, placed her palm on the laser identification panel and turned the handle after she heard the deadbolt click open.

She looked down the hall of identical doorways and walked toward the green light. She entered the office and shut the door behind her, hearing the lock click shut automatically. She took a seat in the only available chair and typed her social security number on the keyboard, pressing the enter key when done. The human face of her computer interface counselor, CO2, appeared on the voice activated monitor welded to the business attired mannequin directly in front of her.

"Alex, how lovely to see you. How are you today?" asked CO2, her smile bright, her air optimistic.

"Wonderful," said Alex sarcastically to the human image. Was CO2 an actress, a human resource representative from a national human resource firm, a computer-generated image, or an employee of Acht? Alex wasn't sure.

"That's good to hear," said CO2 with manufactured optimism, oblivious to or ignoring Alex's tone. "Are you ready for today's interview?"

"Before you tell me about the job, can I get a rundown of the interviews I've been on in the past year?"

"Of course, Alex," said CO2, her computer bank retrieving the stored data. "Starting one year ago, last November, you interviewed with Charlie Jenkins, Vice President of Domestic Distribution. December you spoke with Terry Blandford, Vice President of Jazz/Progressive Music. Your next interview wasn't until February but you met with two people that month, Janie McGrath, Director of AOR Promotion, and Roger Nolte, Vice President Merchandising. In March you spoke with Conrad Fogg, Director of Acht Recording Studios. May was Doni Morgan, Director of Publicity; June you interviewed with Andrew Gray, Vice President of Strategic Planning; August was Paul Skelton, Manager of National Tour Publicity; September was Tim Bristow, Vice President of Video Promotion, and in October you met with Simon Halliday, Director of A&R."

"How many people does that come to?"

"Ten."

"Ten interviews and no job offer. Isn't something wrong?"

CO2 retained her computer-generated calmness. "Alex, finding a job takes time. We've been through this before. We're doing all we can for you, but remember, you are a secretary."

Alex could feel black flow through her hair as her stomach rumbled angrily for the Twinkie she had left behind. When she began interviewing and was passed over, she took the decisions in stride. She wasn't interested enough in the positions and felt other candidates should get the opportunity. But after her fifth rejection, her enthusiasm and optimism waned. Rejection, any kind of rejection, was difficult to handle.

CO2 broke the silence, her corporate smile still in place. "Are we ready for today's interview?"

"Yes," said Alex with resignation. "And Langley's getting worse. He's exploding at least once a week now; I can't take him much longer."

"Good," said CO2 as she ignored or didn't comprehend Alex's usual unattended-to complaint. "Today your interview is with Marty Flanker. He's one of the six Vice Presidents of Marketing here at Acht Records. His secretary has been promoted to Associate Manager of Sales, so he's looking for someone to fill her shoes." CO2 smiled a reassuring, semi-patronizing smile. "He expects a lot from his secretaries, but I'm sure you can handle the job."

A smile crossed Alex's face. Flanker had promoted his secretary to Associate Manager. This could be her chance, the steppingstone job to lead her into management and using her brain. Flanker might be the mentor she had been searching for, the executive who would unlock the door to a successful future. "I can handle it."

"Good, Alex. I have confidence in you." CO2 continued smiling her computer-generated reassuring smile. "He's on the twenty-seventh floor and is waiting for you, so you can go up whenever you're ready."

"Thanks, CO2." Alex stood and moved to the door, the hope of future possibilities lightening her step. When she heard the lock click, she turned the handle. The image of CO2 disappeared from the screen when Alex swung open the door.

As Alex waited for the elevator to take her to her interview, she saw a flash of green and brown zip through her field of vision. Just when she decided she was seeing things, the streak of color returned, let out a short, dry cough, and handed her a cassette. Alex looked at the tall, weedy man and noticed a necklace made of twigs on his green T-shirt and a handful of leaves bulging from his brown jean pockets. She looked at the cassette casing and read 'The Trees'. When she looked up, the Roadrunner had once again disappeared, leaving a vacuum of silence in his wake.

Alex rode the elevator to twenty-seven. The Roadrunner had changed outfits since that morning, an impressive feat for a man who only hours earlier had been covered in blue from head to toe. She walked down the hall and reflexively cringed as she heard a loud crash. She approached Flanker's office just in time to see a temp flying out his door, her eyes wild, her body shaking.

"Hi," said Alex. "I'm here to interview with Marty Flanker."

The temp grabbed her handbag and coat. "Go on in," she said as she started racing down the hall. The temp turned back with a look of concern. "Good luck," she said and then disappeared around the corner.

Alex stepped up and gingerly knocked on the open door.

"What now?!" screamed out from inside the office.

A wave of fear washed over Alex, an instinctual kind of warning, but she pushed aside her feelings, as she had learned to do since starting her job with Langley. She cautiously stepped into Flanker's room. An ashtray whizzed by her right ear and smashed into a thousand pieces against the wall. Alex jumped back through the safety of the office doorway, her hair flaming orange.

"Get in here you idiot!" screamed out from behind the desk.

Alex trembled as she carefully stepped through the door. She ducked just in time. A glass paperweight careened across the room, just missing her skull. The solid hunk of crystal crashed into the wall, the force of its weight leaving a huge hole.

Flanker stopped his arm throwing windup and put his wastebasket down on the desk. "Who the hell are you?"

A nagging feeling settled in Alex's stomach, making her uneasy, but her determination to establish a career, a career she was sure she wanted, forced her to stay. "I'm Alex; I'm here for the interview."

"Oh, dear, do come in," Flanker crooned as he eyed her up and down, approving what he saw.

Marty Flanker jumped off his chair and walked around his standard-sized desk. Alex stared in astonishment as a four foot eleven, beady-eyed, pudgy Napoleon stood in front of her.

"Please, sit down," said Flanker as he pointed to the chair in front of his desk.

Alex sat as Flanker went back around his desk and climbed up on his custom designed booster seat pads. He stared directly at her with his beady little evil eyes, then wordlessly dialed the telephone.

"Cheeseman, it's Flanker. What about the marketing plan we discussed yesterday?"

Alex glanced around Flanker's office as he ignored her and spoke shop with the unknown Cheeseman at the other end of the line. She didn't notice much of interest on the regulation executive ivory walls, just an assortment of autographed photos of Flanker with famous people. He had a set of bookshelves behind his desk, the shelves a mixture of CDs and ceramic and glass figures. She also noticed shards of glass scattered about on the floor.

After twenty minutes of being ignored, Alex was nearing her limit. Secretary or not, her time was also valuable.

Flanker eventually hung up the phone and glanced in Alex's direction. "Tell me about yourself."

Alex took a deep breath and swallowed her anger. "Is there anything in particular you'd like to know?" she asked, dreading the cliché, open-ended question so many interviewers used.

"Whatever you want to tell me."

No matter how many times Alex prepared herself for the question, she was always at a loss with where to begin. "Well, I have a Degree in Communications from Temple University; I'm interested in Marketing and Public Relations. I work for Langley in Legal and Business Affairs; I've been with him for over a year and feel it's time to move into a new position. I'm looking for a job in which I'm challenged.

I don't mind photocopying, typing, and filing, but I need some of my own responsibilities; I need to feel like a part of the company. I only have to be told once to do something. I'm good with finishing tasks and following up on assignments."

Alex warmed up with her background and various slanted half-truths that were specifically directed toward Flanker and the vacant position, so she forged ahead in earnest. "I worked as a coordinator in a public relations firm for almost a year. I enjoy writing, editing, and also organizing events and functions. I'm interested in marketing because I feel it's like publicity, but different enough that it would challenge me, and I would learn another side of the business. Music is one of my major passions in life. When I was younger..."

Alex described her love of music and why she worked in the music industry. As she spoke to Flanker, he stuck his index finger up his nose and wriggled it around.

"...I've always been extremely interested in marketing, and I wouldn't mind one day being a product manager, and I think working for you would give me a lot of experience; I've heard you're very well respected in the company and the music industry as a whole."

Alex continued talking and tried to concentrate on the words coming out of her mouth, but she was mesmerized by the movement in Flanker's nostril. The Vice President of Marketing's finger abruptly stopped, and Alex watched him shut his eyes and scrunch up his face in excited concentration. He slowly removed his finger and extracted a hefty booger.

The snot initially came out hardened and dark green, but as the nose mucous continued to come out of his nostril, it turned lighter and rubberier, until it was downright wet and juicy. Alex stammered over whatever words were deafly falling out of her mouth as she watched the snot extend at least six inches in front of Flanker's nose. She imagined the wet, rubbery booger sliding up from his sinuses, down his nasal passage and out into the room.

The snot freed itself from the Vice President of Marketing's nostril and snapped toward Flanker's finger, like a stretched rubber band contracting back to its original shape. Alex stopped talking and stared speechless at her interviewer as he rolled the snot into a mucous gumball.

When Flanker realized the room was silent, he asked, "Why do you want to work for me?"

"Well," said Alex, watching in growing disgust as Flanker rolled his ball of snot around the table. "I've been told I could learn a lot from you, and that you're a perfect mentor for anyone interested in the music industry." Alex had never heard of Flanker until that day, but she knew ego fibs always helped.

"Do you have any questions for me?"

Alex's eyes were still glued to the piece of snot he was rolling back and forth across his desk. "What are you looking for in an assistant?"

Flanker leaned back and tossed his booger ball up in the air. "A lot of things. I need a secretary to take care of my business, personal and professional, who'll do it with a smile and no errors, with an optimistic attitude. This is not a democracy. I'm not here to cater to your moods and personality; you're here to cater to mine. I expect you to think, to ask intelligent questions, to be able to sense what needs to be done before I tell you.

"And I don't want any excuses about not having a brain. I expect you at your desk ready to work by nine thirty every morning, no exceptions. I want my door unlocked, my lights turned on, and my desk in order before I get in. I expect fresh brewed, hot coffee on my desk every morning within one minute of my arrival. I expect you to do whatever I tell you, with no questions or backtalk, and I don't want to tell you more than once to do something. If you don't like it, I suggest you look elsewhere."

Alex had heard that speech in most of her interviews, so she remained undaunted in her quest to move into a better position. "Is the job promotable?"

Flanker suppressed a chuckle. "Absolutely not. My secretary works for me and only for me. I want your brain in your urn and your backside ready to run at any command I give." He leaned forward and folded his stubby petite hands on the desk, his ball of snot nestled comfortably between his palms. "I know my last secretary was promoted, but she was far and beyond an exception. As a rule, I do not promote."

Alex tried to hide her disappointment. A snot rolling, glass throwing, tyrannical executive was worth working for if the position was promotable, but Alex wasn't sure she could work for the Napoleon of Acht. She forced a smile and lied. "Sounds alright with me."

"Good." Flanker turned back to the telephone and started dialing.

Alex took her cue and stood up. As she walked out, she saw Flanker toss something into the air and catch it in his mouth. She heaved as she heard chewing and a satisfied sigh.

"How did it go?" asked Hellie as Alex stepped off the elevator.

"The usual," said Alex as she walked up to the reception desk, her hair a depressing hue of blue.

Hellie put down her Ticonderoga number two pencil wand and turned away from her mutant sea creatures. "What do you mean?"

Alex recounted her experiences with Flanker as she helped herself to jellybeans from the bowl on Hellie's desk.

"Hi, guys, what's going on?"

Alex turned and saw Zena by her side, clad only in her Victoria Secret red satin slip. Alex didn't want to know what happened to her minidress. Alex noticed sparkling rhinestone earrings swinging from Zena's ears. Alex looked a little closer. They sparkled brilliantly, just like diamonds, but the stones were way too big to be real diamonds. Zena could never afford something like that on her salary. But they looked a lot like real gems.

Zena shook her head, her diamonds swaying to and fro. "What are you guys doing?"

"Nothing," said Alex, deciding she didn't want to know about the earrings. "I just went to an interview and was telling Hellie what happened."

"Oh, wowie, good for you," said Zena. "Who'd you interview with?"

"Someone named Flanker," said Alex.

"Ohhhh," said Zena, her face downcast, her lips pursed in a pout.

"What's that supposed to mean?"

"Nothing, nothing." Zena stepped away from Alex and nervously flicked back her flowing, purple washed black hair.

"Come on, Zena, what's up?" asked Alex.

"Well, I've sort of heard stories about him."

"What kind of stories?" asked Hellie as she adjusted the imitation Chanel silk scarf she wore knotted around her neck.

"I probably shouldn't say," said Zena hesitantly. "They're only stories."

"Who told you?" asked Alex.

"Edwina, Flanker's last assistant," said Zena, her face neither smiling nor pouting. "She used to be my best friend; that is, until she became too important and didn't want to be friends anymore." Zena's tone was wistful yet held no malice. "You see, Edwina got promoted and doesn't have time any more to talk girl talk, or go to the movies, or watch videos over and over again, or even hang out with me."

"What does that have to do with Alex?" asked Hellie as the executive reception phone began ringing. She pushed her voicemail button and let her recording take care of it.

What does Edwina's promotion have to do with Alex?"

"Don't you see?" said Zena. "Edwina got promoted."

"I know Edwina got promoted," said Alex as she became frustrated over Zena's inability to articulate, communicate or otherwise string together a logical thought. "Flanker said she was promoted because she was exceptionally good at her job."

Zena rolled her eyes and giggled. "Blow jobs is what he meant."

"What?" said Alex and Hellie in unison.

Zena's red satin strap slipped off her shoulder as she shrugged with vacant indifference.

"What in the world are you trying to say?" asked Alex heatedly, her hair streaked black and blue.

Zena looked down at her slingback, open-toed, high heeled shoes. "Edwina picked Flanker's nose and gave him blow jobs every morning. Flanker's wife got suspicious, something about chips of nail

30

polish up his nose and lipstick on his underwear, so he had to stop. And he promoted her."

Alex's mouth fell open. "Why didn't she do anything?"

"Do what?" said Zena innocently. "She didn't mind. She always said the road to the boardroom passed through the bedroom." Zena looked around vacantly. "Whatever that means."

"Does that kind of thing still happen?" asked Hellie.

"As long as there are men and women, that kind of thing will probably happen," said Alex. "She ruins it for the rest of us."

Zena slipped her fallen strap back onto her shoulder. "What's she done to you?"

"That's not the point," said Alex. "Any woman using sex to get ahead makes it worse for all women."

"Why should she care about anyone else?" said Zena, a confused look on her face.

"This doesn't bother you, does it?" asked Alex with disbelief.

"Yes, it does. She's not my friend anymore because she's gotten promoted to a better job."

"But it doesn't bother you how she got there?"

Zena shrugged vacantly as Alex continued to stare in disbelief. In the supposed age of equality, the era where women had fought to be treated as an equal, the fact that there were women who used their bodies and not their abilities to get promoted amazed Alex. She used to believe that all women understood the sisterhood, understood they sometimes had to work twice as hard as a man to prove themselves. But Alex realized that as long as there were women who used sex as a bartering tool in the workplace, and as long as men allowed sex to be used, there would never be equality.

"But that's not the point," said Zena, still confused.

"What were you trying to say?"

"I was trying to tell you. Since Edwina left, Flanker's been a madman. He throws things; he screams and yells. He's been through at least a dozen temps, and it's only been a couple of weeks. He went through three in one day. Got one temp right between the eyes. They had to lobotomize and hire her so she wouldn't sue."

"Why doesn't he get fired?" asked Hellie.

"Old Boy Network, Boy's Club, whatever you want to call it," said Alex.

"Oh," replied Hellie. "I've heard about that."

"That's all," said Zena with a wave of her hand as she turned on her heels and sashayed back toward her secretarial suite.

"Is there anything you can do?" asked Hellie once Zena was out of earshot.

Alex sighed and sat down on the edge of Hellie's desk.

"No."

"You're awfully defeatist."

Alex looked at her friend with a sad smile. "I call it being a realist."

"I just can't agree," said Hellie with a tone Alex found slightly unsettling. "There is a way."

Hellie turned back to her aquarium and conducted her mutant sea dwellers, her pencil eraser banging against the glass of the fish tank.

Four

The newly appointed Deity and Ruling Dictator DiMachio always arranged the unannounced corporate executive meetings, so when the Yakadans summoned him and his staff to the boardroom only days after his surprise executive lunch there, and failed to tell him what the meeting concerned, DiMachio was not happy. The Yakadans vowed they wouldn't involve themselves in the day to day running of the company, and DiMachio knew surprise meetings meant meddling.

Deity DiMachio pressed his speakerphone intercom button.

"Heysannah, call the internal surveillance and investigation squad. Start files on the Yakadans. All of them."

"Yes, Mr. DiMachio."

DiMachio barked back. "Did you get the memo about me?"

"Yes, Mr. DiMachio."

"No, I don't think you did," replied the Deity as he stood up, his voice hardening. "I'm Deity now," he screamed into the intercom. "Show me respect!"

"Yes, Deity DiMachio," came back wearily through the phone.

The Deity and Ruling Dictator sat down with a satisfied grunt. He leaned forward in his fur lined gilt trimmed leather throne, his pineapple pockmarked face wrinkled into a scowl.

"Jeremy, you think the aliens found out about the raises and promotions? Think they'll come down on us?"

Jeremy Wickett looked at his boss, silent as always, and frowned along with his master.

DiMachio nodded. "Just what I thought. They can't be trusted. None of them can be trusted."

The Deity pressed his speakerphone intercom and leaned back in his throne. "Heysannah. While you're at it, get the surveillance squad to check the office for bugs."

"Yes, Deity DiMachio."

DiMachio spun his throne around and stared out the window at the glass and concrete buildings that surrounded his corporate kingdom. He glanced at the digital clock on one of the skyscrapers in front of him. Eight minutes past two. He glanced at his watch. Two twelve.

He spun back around and pressed the intercom.

"Yes, Deity DiMachio."

"What time is it?"

"Two twelve."

He clicked off and looked back out the window. Still eight past two. He grunted with irritation and turned back to his desk, his thoughts returning to the meeting. The Yakadans might own the company, but he had to keep control, total control. Domination and power were the key in getting to, and staying at, the top.

The Deity and Ruling Dictator leaned forward in his fur lined gilt trimmed leather throne and turned on his internal television surveillance monitors.

"Oh, shit," escaped his mouth as he stared at the screen.

"Hosannah," he barked into the intercom. "Get me to the boardroom now."

DiMachio and Jeremy Wickett were chauffeured one floor up and entered the boardroom where all major company decisions had been made over the years. They walked casually toward their throne at the end of the antique mahogany conference room table, an air of executive disinterest masking their disbelief at the sight surrounding them. The ceiling to floor rich red drapes were untied and drawn, forcing the sunlight to stay outside. The overhead lights were dimmed and cast an almost candlelit glow around the room.

And before their eyes mingled several dozen green-tinged alien Elvis Presley impersonators, or El-Yaks, resplendent in full, late period Elvis Las Vegas attire. They stood proudly, their full black wigs pulled down awkwardly over their squarish heads, their bushy black sideburns glued securely in place. They each wore a jewel studded white polyester jumpsuit, unbuttoned and showing off clumps of black hair glued onto green chests. All had a silk scarf thrown casually around their neck. Some Yakadans had ornately jeweled capes thrown around their shoulders, others wore large, metal-framed tinted glasses, and others wore wide multicolored jeweled belts with large square studded buckles.

Langley, Derby, Jiglio, Weena, and Skeater sat nervously in their unofficially official chairs. As DiMachio passed Weena he paused. He leaned over her right shoulder and ran his finger across the table in front of her. Satisfied all traces of flesh had been removed, DiMachio straightened and weaved through the small throng of jewel encrusted, white polyester jumpsuits to his throne. There was an air of anxious expectancy filling the room, an electricity running through the mixture of beings assembled around him.

"Oh, my," said Weena as one of her fingers bounced and rolled off the mahogany table.

The El-Yak to her right flipped his jewel studded cape back over his shoulder and bent down, kindly retrieving her detached digit. He held the finger out to Weena.

"Oh, my," Weena repeated as her ear and another finger fell to the table.

She reached deep into her black canvas shoulder bag briefcase and pulled out her prescription bottle of Xanax, popping two of the mind-numbing pills into her mouth. She then pulled out her tube of Medical Repair and Reattachment Glue and began piecing herself back together.

DiMachio watched his Senior Senior Executive President of Media Relations as she expertly reglued herself, getting each part back in its proper place in a matter of seconds. The more the El-Yak tried to help by handing back her body parts, the faster her body fell to the table and the more Xanax she popped into her mouth.

DiMachio pulled out his executive mini-cassette tape recorder and placed it in front of his mouth.

"Heysannah," he said as discreetly as a Deity could speak. "If Weena ever loses all body parts at the same time, we might have to replace her. Have candidates ready." He glanced in Weena's direction and saw her eye pop out of its socket. "No one who loses body parts. And no one from inside."

DiMachio clicked off his recorder. A Deity had to be prepared. And no use wasting time with internal employees. They had in-house allies, corporate friends, and political ties. Fresh blood was easier to train in the DiMachio way of thinking.

Deity and Ruling Dictator DiMachio sat in his fur lined gilt trimmed boardroom throne and nodded a silent greeting to everyone in the room. Jeremy, as always, was at his side. El-Yak's were scattered about everywhere.

DiMachio pulled out his cell phone and dialed.

"Highs today in the 50's. Scattered clouds. Moderate winds. A look toward the weekend shows..."

DiMachio grunted and nodded, the phone close to his ear, his expression serious. He clicked off and dialed another number.

"Hosannah, Heysannah, whoever you are. Messages."

"Yes, Deity DiMachio. Your dry cleaning is ready. Mrs. Deity DiMachio asked you to pick it up. The book you ordered has arrived at the store. Save The Children wants you to speak at their charity dinner. That's all for now, Deity DiMachio."

"Go pick up my dry cleaning. Bring it back to the office. Send a messenger to pick up the book. Say no to the dinner, but with the usual excuses."

"Yes, Deity DiMachio."

DiMachio clicked off. Having a mobile phone meant a man was not only a man, he was also a high-powered executive man. The Deity phoned people from restaurants, elevators, department stores, anywhere other people might get a glimpse of him. He phoned his twin assistants, the Doublemint girls of rock, Hosannah and Heysannah, every morning from his car when he was less than five minutes from the office, impressing both himself and the driver. After all, he was the Deity of the company, and DiMachio enjoyed flexing his manly extension and reminding people of his stature.

The boardroom doors swung open. In walked three more El-Yak's, their faces greener than usual, their mouths twisted into what DiMachio guessed was a smile. Smiling didn't seem to come naturally to the aliens. Behind them a nine-foot, dinosaur-like egg rolled in on a motorized dolly, followed by a fourth and final El-Yak carrying the controls that guided the egg. The creamy metallic shell glowed under the boardroom's soft lighting as it mechanically rolled to the front of the room.

Anyone still standing immediately found a seat. The Head Yakadan, distinguishable only by the triangular, dark metallic green pin attached to the lapels of the most ornate Elvis cape in the room, stood next to the egg, an El-Yak on either side.

"Yak, yak, yak-yak, yak-yak-yak-yak, yak," started the Head Yakadan. Verbal speech did not exist on Yaka; the Yakadans communicated through an intricate inner sonar system, similar to dolphins, and they could only utter a noise like the word 'yak'. When the Yakadans first made contact with Earth, some ten years earlier, they had been concerned their plans to do business with the planet would be hampered if they couldn't communicate verbally, until a Yakadan historian uncovered research done around earth time 1964.

The Autobureat, the one and only ruling body on the planet Yaka, had been fascinated with the British invasion and had sent scores of Yakadans to Earth to secretly observe the phenomenon firsthand. While there, several females carried out their assigned mission and got pregnant by a few members of Fab Four impersonator bands. Yakadan scientists studied the offspring to see if any of the children could be trained to recreate the poppy, head bobbing tunes, but, alas, they all seemed incapable of making those fun-loving rock and roll sounds that years earlier had entered Yakadan space.

With great sadness, the scientists concluded that the human ability to sing and make foot stomping, dance inducing music could not be passed on to their race, so the TerraYaks, half-Yakadan half-Earth creatures, were cast aside and looked upon as third-class citizens. When the Yakadan historian presented this information to the Autobureat, the ruling body immediately rounded up the TerraYaks and their families and put them in special training camps, teaching them English from satellite transmissions of Elvis Presley movies. To the Autobureat's delight, the TerraYaks were able to learn the language with a minimum of difficulty, thus elevating the TerraYaks' status from that of third-class plebeians to highly respected members of society.

After the Head El-Yak had yakked himself out, unable to communicate with the inferior beings in front of him, the TerraYak took over, speaking in flawless English what the Head Yakadan sonically told him.

"Good morning, and welcome to this special gathering," began the TerraYak in a very un-Elvis monotone voice, an audible manifestation of the uniformity in their lives. "We asked you here to unveil our latest creation, the latest in music that will not only allow us to sell millions of records, it will reinforce Acht's reputation of quality and good music."

Langley, Jiglio, Weena, and Derby looked at each other puzzled. Even DiMachio was thrown off slightly. They had never considered the possibility that the Yakadans might have an interest in music; they had assumed the aliens had taken over Acht in order to make money. Maybe there was more to these foreign creatures than the color of green.

All eyes followed the finger of the TerraYak as he pointed to the metallic egg. "May I introduce you to the next superstar on Acht Records."

The El-Yak with the control panel stepped forward slightly and pressed a button. The metal egg slowly began to unfold, the creamy shell peeling back like the petals on a wilting flower. Everyone strained to see the contents, the El-Yak's anxious with the knowledge of what the egg held, the humans expecting a new piece of audio equipment or high-tech gadgetry. When the shell peeled back fully and rested on the floor, a spotlight focused on the darkened contents.

An audible gasp vibrated throughout the room. Standing inside the shell, on a platform coated in gold, was a seven-foot human, tall and solid, but not too muscular. He stood motionless, his sculpted hands down by his side, his head bent forward with eyes closed. His skin was silky smooth like a baby's, and almost dove white. He had black pompadoured hair and soft, clean cut all American features. The figure was dressed in a fitted black leather biker jacket and tight black leather pants, and on his feet were standard black biker boots.

The TerraYak interrupted the shocked silence. "Before I give you background, you must all sign the Intergalactic Privacy and Confidentiality form my associate will hand out."

One of the seated El-Yak's pulled a stack of papers from his briefcase and passed them out to the humans. DiMachio began to protest but had second thoughts. More important issues would arise over the next couple of years as the transition of ownership was fully implemented and finalized, issues that might affect the Deity's control over his company.

DiMachio read the paper. The agreement was a standard confidentiality form which stated that each person who signed would not discuss, reveal or otherwise make public any of the information discussed during the meeting, as well as impart any information regarding the Yakadans or any of their technologies and/or discoveries. The penalty was immediate termination and an infringement lawsuit. DiMachio briefly considered consulting with Langley, but when he glanced over and saw his Senior Senior Executive President of Business Affairs and Law, and General Counsel, signing his own form without question or negotiation, the Deity followed suit, putting both his and Jeremy Wickett's names on the paper.

As soon as everyone signed, the El-Yak with the briefcase collected the forms and verified that proper signatures were on each. He reached for his official earth government stamp and quickly notarized each piece of paper.

When everything was in order, and the signed and notarized forms were safely back in the El-Yak's briefcase, the TerraYak motioned toward the giant male figure and resumed speaking. "The Autobureat, our planet's government, has been funding research for cloning and robotics for centuries. When we began receiving your satellite and radio transmissions, and heard what you call music, we decided we had to have our own. To our disappointment, we cannot recreate the sounds you make, so we invested many years into finding a way to make our own musicians and singers. Our research continues, and it will take many years before we perfect a Yakadan music machine, but we've successfully created a humanoid clonebot that can be programmed to our musical needs."

The TerraYak stepped closer to the Yakadan-made creature. "This is a Y1K, a half robot, half clone, one we call a clonebot. Our research and development staff nicknamed him Adam, after the first Earth man. He is part robot, but he has been cloned from human tissue, so he will bleed if cut, eat and drink like the rest of us, and so on. Y1K is human in most respects, except the robot parts regenerate his human tissue so he should never age or die. The internal parts might eventually wear out, but we're confident we can replace the machinery when that happens."

The TerraYak attempted a smile. His mouth twisted out of its natural straight line as his Elvis wig slipped back on his squarish head.

He tugged on his artificial hair, pulling it down over the squarish corners of his forehead, and adjusted it back into place.

"There is one characteristic of this type of clonebot that is important to remember. Adam is not like robots you are probably familiar with through your television programs and science fiction books. He is programmed with specific capabilities and characteristics which are fed into his internal computer. We did not program actual commands into him; we programmed propensities and characteristics that will lead Adam to perform the commands you tell him. These clonebots can think and reason."

Everyone nodded. DiMachio was intrigued but still somewhat cautious. "What did you program in this clonebot?"

"Adam is a rock star," said the TerraYak. "We've programmed the propensity to sing, play guitar, and write songs through our genetic cloning procedures. We've also programmed in the need to be loved, and with that need will come undying devotion to his owner, which is you and your staff. We kept his IQ low so he wouldn't become too intelligent."

The TerraYak glanced at the Head El-Yak who nodded slightly, his upper lip struggling to curl upward. The TerraYak continued.

"Hundreds of Yakadans invested their lives to bring us this moment, and we summoned you here to witness the birth of a new phase of humanity. Adam will not know he is different from anyone else, and you must not reveal his true nature to anyone, even to him. Only the people in this room know the truth."

All businesses had their dirty little secrets, and DiMachio was often exposed to top secret and highly confidential material. As long as silence benefited him, his lips were sealed. And DiMachio was confident his executives would also remain silent, their fear of him outweighing any temptation to talk.

The Head El-Yak and the TerraYak stepped back from Adam. The TerraYak turned to the table. "Ladies and gentlemen, let the birth begin."

The El-Yak with the control panel walked behind the clonebot and cut open a one-inch square in the back of Adam's neck. He removed a circuit from the control panel and inserted it into the Y1K. He replaced the skin and secured it with a generous amount of Medical

Repair and Reattachment Glue, making sure the glue was evenly distributed so the skin would never loosen. The alien stepped back to the front of the clonebot and took his place next to the Head El-Yak. He raised the control panel.

The Head El-Yak closed his eyes and bowed slightly. He opened them as the control panel was ceremoniously lowered and held in front of him. The only movement in the executive conference room was the Head El-Yak's arm as it reached for the red button on the panel. His finger made contact.

The boardroom was thrown into frozen blackness. Machine parts began moving, the sound bouncing off the silence and creating a deafening roar. When the noise stopped, tiny white spotlights switched on from inside the metallic eggshell. Their beam focused on the man machine's face, illuminating and distorting his features in ghostlike shadows. The spotlights rose over the head of the clonebot and stopped when they came in contact with the mirrored disco ball that had risen from the shell of the egg. The ball began to rotate, spinning dots of light on everyone and everything in the room while music blared from speakers located under the feet of the clonebot. Random songs from Elvis Presley's *Viva Las Vegas* pulsated off the walls and through the bodies of each person present. The El-Yaks went crazy, posing and dancing to the music as best a person from a nonmusical society could.

Skeater tugged on his ear, turning off his internal music. He immediately began jamming to some of the most influential rock and roll sounds of the twentieth century. When "Viva Las Vegas" came over the speakers, the A&R executive couldn't help singing along while the room of El-Yaks thrust and ground their pelvises at each other.

The music stopped. The lights went out as quickly as they had come on, throwing the room into blinded silence. As blood pressure began to drop, thick clouds of dry ice poured out of the golden platform on which Adam stood, spiraling and curling throughout the room. Colored concert lights shone from the ceiling in front of the clonebot, silhouetting him black against the blue, red, and yellow glaring beams. Electric guitars pierced the air, wailing and whining in lengthy guitar solos, sounds reminiscent of the days heavy metal dominated the airwaves. The guitars stopped, replaced by a two-minute drum solo, surprisingly rhythmic and not too torturous.

When the noise finally ended, muzak cover versions of every bad song ever written poured simultaneously out of the speakers. The white spotlights redirected their beam onto the disco ball, the dots of light spinning faster and faster around the room. Colored spotlights blinked and pulsated harder and harder as they tried to cut through the billowing ice smoke. The heat intensified until the walls began to sweat. The music became louder and louder, the lights spun faster and faster, and the heat became hotter and hotter until every executive and El-Yak were up on their feet, their bodies throbbing and ready to explode.

When the crowd had been taken to that final point where sight and sound and all other senses are so overwhelmed they overload and prepare to shut down, the music stopped. Everyone teetered off balance as the room was hurled into darkness. Weena swooned and fell to the ground, her weight creating a tremor that nearly felled the clonebot. The spotlights came on and slowly focused on the Y1K. Through the silence came a beat, softly at first, but growing louder and louder, the sound of a bass drum. Through the heartbeat of the sound came a guitar, three chord simplicity, bringing rhythm to the beat. Heads bobbed unconsciously as a bass guitar and drums joined in, creating the simple rhythms and infectious sounds of early rock and roll.

Without warning, the clonebot's head jerked upright and his eyes bolted open, staring directly at Weena sitting on the floor. She fainted backward, her mouth agape and close to falling off. The man machine slowly began to clench and unclench his tightened fists, twist and turn his stiffened wrists. The music grew louder with each movement the Y1K made. He raised his hands toward his face and looked down at them, his expression blank and uncomprehending. He turned his head right, then left, stretching, focusing, learning how to use his muscles and move his limbs.

The lights intensified and directed their rays solely on him while the music reached an earsplitting level. The clonebot blinked, then involuntarily raised his arms over his head, his fists clenched and interlocked as he assumed the essential Roger Daltrey rock stance. The music built and built until the robot forcefully lowered his arms and opened his mouth, his diaphragm exploding.

"Mama," squeaked the next international mega super rock star.

Five

"ALEX!" flew out of Langley's door into Alex's face.

She automatically jumped up, grabbed her steno pad and pen, and hurried into Langley's office. She sat on her steno stool, a two-foot-high wooden seat Langley had ordered her to use after he decided she looked too comfortable in his guest chairs.

"Letter to Bret Horowitz, entertainment lawyer."

Alex flipped to a blank page and readied her pen.

"Regarding Parmazeen. Dear Bret, in reference to your recent letter regarding Parmazeen, we have considered your proposal and are willing to offer the following terms. New paragraph. Term. Parmazeen."

Alex cringed as she busily scribbled. He said it three times, now was her only chance.

"Langley, I'm sorry, but can you spell that?"

"What?" he barked, his cigarette falling out of his mouth.

Alex squirmed uncomfortably in her seat as her hand trembled. "Parmazeen. I've never heard the name before and want to get the spelling right."

Langley's fists pounded hard on his desk, putting out the lit cigarette that had started to smolder on the papers scattered about. "Did I ask you a question?! Did I ask you to speak?"

"But I'm just trying to spell…"

Langley stood up and leaned toward Alex, his fists clenched. "That's not what I asked you!" His eyes bulged from their sockets. "I asked you if I asked a question!"

Alex looked down and clutched her steno pad, shaking with fear.

"ANSWER ME!"

"N…no."

Langley's fists slammed onto his desktop. "That's right, I didn't!"

"But..."

"God damn it! I've had enough of you and your insubordination! I've told you NEVER to speak unless spoken to, never to look at me unless absolutely necessary, and to act like you don't exist when you're around me!"

Alex knew she was still in his office, knew he was still screaming at her, but she felt herself slipping inside her head to a safe place where he couldn't reach her. She forced her face muscles to relax, numbed herself to any feelings or emotions, and sat in front of him like a zombie. Alex remained paralyzed in her chair, not thinking, not feeling, not being.

"I'M TALKING TO YOU!"

Alex looked up and saw Langley standing in front of her, shaking with uncontrollable rage. His left fist was clenched and up by his side. He turned and kicked the bottom of his desk with such force he cracked the wood. He looked back at her, his face purple with rage, and opened his mouth to scream. But instead of words, the veins on both sides of his neck exploded. Blood spewed out and shot across the room in both directions. He leaned into Alex's face, his blood gushing all over her.

"YOU'RE FIRED! Get the hell out of my sight and don't ever come back!"

Langley started back toward his chair.

"You can't just fire me," Alex muttered.

He wheeled around, pure hate filling his eyes as blood continued to spew out of his neck. "YES I CAN! Go ask Winkle!"

Alex shakily stood up, her legs trembling. This isn't happening, she said to herself, this is some kind of nightmare.

Langley pointed to the door, his clothes now soaked with blood. "GET THE HELL OUT OF HERE!"

Alex didn't know how she got out of the office, but she found herself at her desk, her body trembling, her mind numb. She watched her brain floating dormant in its nutrient juice. Maybe it would be better if she kept it out forever. No, maybe it would be better if she put it in. Maybe things would make more sense. Alex leaned over and grabbed her cerebrum urn, shoving her brain in and zipping up her head. A thought briefly danced across her mind that these days she seemed to be thinking almost the same with or without her brain, but she quickly pushed the idea aside.

Alex wiped off the blood that had soaked her as she tried to sort through the scattered thoughts racing frantically around her brain. It was as if her mind and her body had taken on a life of their own, and Alex had become a mere observer. She put down the bloodied paper towels and reached into her drawer, grabbing a snack-sized Snickers bar. She tore off the wrapper and shoved the entire candy into her mouth.

Okay, she thought to herself as she chewed her anger. I have to get control. He fired me, that's a fact. I'm on the unemployment line. Again. It'll probably take a year to find a job. So-called friends will stop calling because I can't do anything for them or give them anything. I'll have to deal with that. I'll have no money to go out, just enough for the bills. But I'll get by. Alex swallowed and let out a sigh. But it's that loneliness all over again, that sense of not belonging anywhere, the feeling of having no purpose. She reflexively grabbed another piece of candy and quickly ate it.

But wait. Winkle. Langley said to ask Winkle. Alex thumbed through her corporate directory and found his room number. She headed to his office, her hair a mixture of ill green, anger black, apprehensive orange and stress magenta.

*

"So, Alex, Langley has fired you."

"Yes."

"Hmm."

Winkle thumbed through Alex's personnel file. "Would you like to tell me what happened?"

Alex looked at the head of the Equal Employment Opportunity division and knew she didn't like him. He was ordinary and unassuming, a nonthreatening kind of person that would be invisible walking down the street. His skin was fair, his hair light brown, his features plain and indistinguishable. He was an out of focus picture, and something about him bothered her. Alex wasn't sure if it was his smug, executive look, or the feeling of boredom and disinterest she sensed coming from his side of the desk, but there was something about him she didn't like.

45

"There's not much to say. I was taking dictation, asked him to spell something, and he lost his temper and fired me."

Winkle looked at her through his unfocussed wire-framed glasses. "That's all there is to it?"

"Well," said Alex as a feeling of dizziness came over her. "He's always yelling at me and exploding blood vessels for no reason. I've told personnel for over a year, and they keep telling me to hold on, that they'll help me get another job. But I've been to a lot of interviews and no one's hired me."

Winkle's tone was calm and unassuming. "And you think that's Langley's fault?"

"I don't know whose fault it is. All I know is I've been to a lot of interviews and no one has offered me a job."

"Hmm."

Winkle leaned back in his chair, almost blending in with the blandness of his office.

"And why have you come to see me?"

Alex's head was still spinning, her mind now unable to focus. The dullness of Winkle and his office was paralyzing Alex's already numbed mind. She began to feel almost hypnotized as she heard herself say, "Langley told me to. He fired me for no reason and told me he could. He said if I didn't believe him to ask you. So, I'm asking."

Winkle leaned forward, his average-sized hands resting on his desk.

"Do you have documentation?"

"Documentation?" was all she could say.

Winkle looked down and shuffled the papers on his desk, avoiding Alex. His tone remained calm and bland. "Yes. Threatening memos, tape recordings. Something concrete."

"No," somehow came out of her mouth.

"I see." Winkle came into focus as a small smile played around the corners of his mouth. He sat straight and adjusted his glasses, looking much more alive. His voice became clear and businesslike. "Well, it's not generally company policy, but there's a law in New York called Termination at Will. It means an employee can get fired for any

46

reason. We tend not to enforce it here at Acht because we care about our employees, but when an executive and an assistant have a problem, it's one person's word against another. And when it comes to that, we side with the executive."

Alex stared at Winkle. His change of tone cleared away the confusion clouding her mind. Equal employment opportunity must not include the support staff.

"I can't believe it," she said.

Winkle was sharp and completely in focus. "I'm sorry, but there's nothing I can do. But he must terminate you in writing."

Alex was flabbergasted. "What?"

"You have to go back and get a termination letter from him."

Alex stood up, her hair a mixture of black and magenta. "I don't believe this place."

Winkle shrugged his shoulders, his smugness covered in ice. "No one forced you to work here."

                                        *

Tears of anger and hurt stung at Alex's eyes as she sat at her desk and packed her personal things into an empty box.

I should do something, she thought as she opened a desk drawer and began throwing pens, pencils, paper clips, tape, staples, and anything she could find into her box. I should walk into his office and tell him off. Sue him. Throw a fit. Just do something.

Alex sighed as a tear she'd been fighting back escaped down her cheek. It's not worth it. He wins. I'm too tired to care. It just doesn't matter anymore. She grabbed a piece of candy and absentmindedly put it in her mouth.

Alex finished filling her box, took a deep breath, and dried her eyes. She didn't care what he did or where she ended up. She walked into Langley's office.

He was sitting at his blood encrusted desk, reddened surgical gauze wrapped so tightly around his neck it looked more like a tourniquet than a bandage. His head was purple from the lack of proper blood flow. Stray pieces of gauze stuck out wildly from his neck. He was writing on a tablet of paper, two red-stained cigarettes dangling from his mouth.

Alex spoke. "Langley, I need my termination in writing. They won't let me go without it."

Langley pushed the papers he had been working on toward Alex. He reached for the closest paper on his desk and stared at the page. His voice was calm, like it always was after an especially huge eruption. "I'll think about it. Type that up."

"What?" asked Alex, sure she had heard wrong.

Langley sucked on his cigarette and continued to avoid eye contact. "Type that letter. It has to go out today."

Alex stammered, "B...but you fired me."

Langley remained calm. "I said I'd think about it. Now get to your desk and start typing. And get someone to clean this office."

Alex picked up the pile of blood-stained papers. Her brain stopped working and no thoughts would form. Like a programmed robot, she sighed and carried the papers toward the door. As Alex walked out of Langley's office, her last pieces of hope started to slip away. And she knew if hope went, she would too.

Six

One week and twenty-five meetings after the alien Elvis hatching, Skeater found himself at the conference room table yet again, surrounded by his fellow executives. The routine had become a bore.

Weena held up her bandaged hand. "I called the meeting so I'm in charge. Let's get started."

Skeater sighed and tugged his ear. He kept the volume low, in case Weena surprised them all and had something important to say. He watched as she shuffled her papers, banged them on the table, grunted, and tried to look threateningly authoritative as everyone ignored her. It was a far cry from the day she had chaired her first meeting.

Weena had recently been promoted to the Senior Vice President of Media Relations position, due to the somewhat suspicious, though unfortunate and untimely, death of the entire media relations department while on a company-funded trip to Vail, Colorado, only months earlier. The entire department had taken to the ski slopes for an afternoon of fun and relaxation, but the day turned into a living nightmare when Weena lost control and veered off the ski slope, slamming face first into a pine tree. The force of the impact, and the subsequent earth tremor from Weena's fall, loosened the powdery snow that had been falling for days and created an avalanche of such magnitude that everyone on the slope was swept away under tons of snow, their bodies never found. Weena was the only one from her department to survive, her life saved by the forest she had accidentally skied into as the thicket and trees surrounding her stopped the snow from burying her alive.

"Everyone, be quiet. We're wasting time and there's a lot to do."

Weena opened the plastic bottle next to her papers and swallowed two Xanax.

Skeater silently shook his head. Weena began, her fast talking, nasal voice even more piercing than usual, but no one heard a word.

They were too busy staring. When she waved her right hand for emphasis, her index finger flew through the air and nearly hit Derby in the eye. When she waved her left hand, her thumb soared across the room and smacked Langley in the neck, lodging into an ever-present mound of coagulated blood. The room became filled with flying digits, and everyone ducked to avoid being hit with a piece of Weena. When she had lost almost all her fingers, her ears, her nose, and all her hair, her body began to make a juicy gurgling sound. Her face and arms began to bubble with festering red boils, the red mounds pulsating and moving across her skin.

The executives were horrified, yet perversely mesmerized, by the growing, throbbing red boils that had taken on a life of their own. The mounds quickly grew into mountains. In the back of the executives' minds, they knew they should evacuate, but they were all glued to their seats. The gurgling sounds became louder. The mounds grew larger and larger. When Weena sneezed, it was all over. The boils exploded like volcanoes. Mountains of trapped pus and blood spewed forth over the entire room, covering everybody and everything. Even Derby stopped eating when the food he'd brought into the meeting became coated with white, oozing pus and thick, red blood.

Weena expertly reglued herself and acted as if nothing had happened. She pulled out a wad of tissues and wiped the pus and blood off her arms. "Listen. The quicker we start, the quicker we're out of here."

"Then let's get started," Jiglio barked.

Weena straightened her papers and avoided eye contact. "First, we have to figure out a name for that robot. Adam isn't right. We need something better, something more original. Something people will remember."

"Why?" asked Derby.

"Adam. First man. Garden of Eden. Suggests nudity, sins, banishment. It's not good for the robot's image." Weena shrugged her shoulders. "And DiMachio doesn't like the name. So, we change it."

Weena reshuffled the papers in front of her. "We need something memorable, something catchy, something manly, showing strength. Something people will latch onto, think of in their sleep, want to identify with, someone they'd want to be.

"How about John?" asked Derby.

"No," came the unanimous reply.

"Paul," said Derby.

"No," resounded throughout the room.

"George?" asked Derby.

"No!" echoed back again.

"Ringo!"

"Hmmm," everyone said as the executives glanced at each other. No one wanted to say it, no one wanted to be the first to admit...

"No, we can't," said Weena, sadness coloring her words.

The executives were disappointed. No one wanted to admit Ringo had been their favorite, but each had secretly hoped the honor would be bestowed.

"Perhaps we need a subcommittee to discuss the name problem in more detail," said Derby.

Jiglio glared at him from across the table. "This meeting is to decide his name."

"Yes, but," said Derby, his ornate silver fork tucked behind his ear and trembling like a divining rod. "Perhaps we should divide into subgroups. We could come up with lists of suggestions and meet again and vote on the name we want."

"Not a bad idea," said Weena as she snuck a lustful glance in Derby's direction. "It could help us focus."

The boil on Jiglio's forehead reddened and began to throb. "We don't need ten meetings and subgroups to decide on a name."

"But if we're not having any luck now," said Derby.

"No!"

"Alright," said Derby, his silver fork drooping sadly on his ear. "How about Mickey?"

"No."

Skeater looked around him with growing disbelief at what he was beginning to see. He had worked at Acht for five years but had kept to himself as much as possible, going to shows, listening to music, doing what an A&R person should do by looking for good music to sign to the label. But recently, in the past few months, he started to feel the pressure of the corporation, the struggle to be creative in an environment not suited for creativity, the endless string of meetings and more meetings, the mountains of paperwork. He was beginning to feel distanced, beginning to open his eyes to what was going on around him. And he didn't like what he was seeing.

He slipped his hand under his dark blue cotton pullover sweater and turned up the volume on the music player attached to his stomach. He listened contentedly for several minutes, until a sharp pain stabbed him in the forehead. He jumped and opened his eyes. Skeater put his hand to his face and felt a Bic ballpoint sticking out of his skin.

He tugged on his ear and turned off his music. "Hey, man, what's going on?"

He yanked the pen from his forehead. When he looked down, he saw another Bic ballpoint dangling from his ferret's neck.

"Hey, Skat wasn't bothering anyone."

Weena was standing, her hands in fists on her large hips. "Skeater, stop listening to music and pay attention. We've got serious work to do."

*

Skeater caressed Skat's fur and removed the pen, remembering the nightmare that had taken his best friend's life. It was during the Grammy Awards, the year bad disco had made a comeback, though the second time around was even worse because Skeater and Skat knew what they would have to endure. Skat had been acting edgy all day, sniffing in the corners of the apartment for no apparent reason and walking around in circles.

When the award ceremony began, group after group of semi- or untalented musicians had taken the stage, one hit unwonders, accepting awards for music that could only be called bad. Skat had become downright fidgety, his nose twitching nervously, his little paws shaking. When the Disco Divas took the stage to perform, Skat lost complete control. He ran crazily around the room, bashing into furniture and ramming into any object in front of him. He leapt over the coffee table in a panic and headed straight for the far wall.

Skeater couldn't react in time and watched helplessly as Skat ran headfirst into the electrical socket, his tiny nose becoming lodged in the top, third prong electrical hole. Skeater heard the jolt kill Skat, and the smell of electrically expelled excrement filled the apartment permanently. Skeater had to move shortly after his pet's death, his mind unable to forget the two horrors he witnessed the day disco music had once again been legitimized and honored.

Skeater was unable to bury his best friend, unable to let go and remember the memories, so he had the ferret stuffed and mounted. Once Skat had been cleaned up and stuffed for eternity, Skeater almost forgot he was dead. He carried Skat with him everywhere. The music man even bought his ferret a pair of tiny custom-made aviator sunglasses exactly like his own and permanently attached them to his furry little head.

"Skeater," said Weena, bringing the A&R executive back to the meeting. "Pay attention. We're trying to figure out a name for that robot we saw come to life last week, and we need everyone's help, including yours."

Skeater looked around the room. He was met with indifferent eyes. "What's up?"

"We need a name," repeated Weena, her tone nearing exasperation, the fingernail on the pinky of her right-hand dangling precariously.

"Well," said Skeater. "He's certainly Big. Why don't you just call him Big?"

"Big?!" exclaimed Weena. "What kind of name is that?"

"Wait a minute, Weena," said Langley through the wall of smoke rising from several burning cigarettes in his overflowing ashtray. "Think about it. Big." Langley pulled a fresh cigarette out of his pack and lit up. He exhaled toward the ceiling and continued. "It might work. It's unusual; it gives the impression of bigness. You know, big star, big man, big everything. Women can comment on how Big he is. Big is Big in every respect."

Langley, Derby, Weena, and Jiglio looked at each other, letting the name sink in while they waited for someone to comment.

Jiglio was the first to speak up. "He's got a point."

Derby nodded in agreement.

"Great idea, Langley," said Weena. "I think you got it."

Skeater stood and picked up Skat.

"Where do you think you're going?" said Weena.

"Hey, man, you named your rock star. The meeting's over. I've got music to listen to."

Weena pointed to Skeater's chair. "Sit. We still need marketing, publicity, and promotion plans, as well as a bio."

Skeater reluctantly sat down and placed Skat back on the conference room table.

"Media Relations is next." Weena put down the meeting agenda her secretary had typed, retyped, and edited ten times, the agenda no one else had a copy of but which her assistant had spent half a day correcting and editing.

"That's me." Weena reached into her bag and pulled out a thick pile of papers. She dropped it on the table. "We'll do the superstar media plan. It's been done before successfully, so we'll do it again. All major press, TV, and radio. The usual plan for a superstar."

Weena picked up her pen and checked off an item on her agenda. "Image is next."

"Has anyone heard his music yet?" asked Skeater half asleep.

"What does that matter?" said Jiglio.

"What do you mean, what does that matter?" said Skeater, wondering what had taken him so long to see what he was surrounded by. "If you don't know what kind of music he makes, how can you create an image?"

"Skeater, get out of the dark ages. It's the nineties," said Jiglio. "We create his image first; the music follows. We're creating his music too, remember?"

Skeater didn't reply. Music used to create an image, not just money for record executives. How many more mediocre superstars could be forced down the public's throats? Skeater longed for the days when music was more about music and not solely a corporate, money making, business machine.

"Image," said Weena again. "Any ideas?"

The executives looked blankly at each other. Weena reached into her bag and pulled out another stack of papers. She dropped them onto the media plan. "How about the Soft Rock Ballad Plan? I've got one here."

All heads nodded in approval.

Skeater had no desire to participate, so he looked around the table and said nothing as the other executives created a musical caricature.

"What about sales and marketing?" asked Weena.

Derby reached to the floor and put a spiral bound book on his desk. "The usual for a superstar."

All heads nodded in agreement. Skeater knew there was no point arguing. He learned quickly that corporate executives would only do what had been done before. The plans were all written; they only had to fill in names and dates. No work got done at meetings like this. They were held to let the executives believe they were doing something.

Weena scribbled notes on her papers. Without looking up, she said, "Promotion?"

Jiglio stared at Weena, but her body parts remained intact. "Superstar promotion plan," was all he said, not bothering to add to the stacks of paper piling up on the conference room table.

In under an hour the executives had filled in the blanks in their standard marketing plans, plans that were used over and over, year in and year out.

"What's left for us to do?" asked Langley, his neck scabs picked, the wounds reopened but not oozing, the hardened blood clots flicked under his chair and onto the floor as near to his colleagues' feet as he dared.

Weena looked over her agenda. "We have to figure out a background for the biography. We need to create a history and give Big a past that people will believe."

"Any suggestions?"

"That's your job, not ours," said Jiglio with a note of disgust.

Weena opened her bag and pulled out a two-foot stack of papers. She dropped them onto the table.

"We have a lot of choices, but I say let's go for the Tarzan persona. Rough on the outside, a pussycat inside."

She rummaged through the pile and pulled out a short stack. Holding it up for everyone, she said, "Here it is. Lost his family at a young age. Grew up in South America in a small village in the mountains. And so on and so on. It's all written out."

Skeater watched the other executives nod in agreement. He pulled on his ear and turned up his music. He picked up Skat and walked out of the room, sickened by the self-congratulatory nature of executives who do nothing.

Seven

From the day Big was hatched in the executive boardroom on the thirty-seventh floor in the corporate monolith called Acht, DiMachio knew the next international mega super rock star was his retirement nest egg. The clonebot could be manipulated, trained, developed, and turned into whatever he wanted him to be, and DiMachio realized Big's fame and popularity would only increase his own power and executive pocketbook.

Deity and Ruling Dictator DiMachio began Big's career by putting the clonebot under an exclusive contract with the record company. He was concerned the Yakadans might turn greedy and keep Big's royalties for themselves, and he was also worried another record company might somehow try to steal the soon-to-be international mega super rock star away from him, so he put Big under an eternity-long deal with Acht Records, the first contract of such length ever offered by a record company and almost knowingly agreed to by an artist.

The contract was the standard sixty-plus pages, with slight alterations and amendments to tailor the deal to Big's unique circumstances and DiMachio's whims. DiMachio made sure the contract had the standard twenty-five percent packaging deduction, fifteen percent free goods clause, and all other hidden record company deductions that were common in artist contracts.

In addition, Deity DiMachio made himself producer of all Big's recordings, in perpetuity, and gave himself producer points of three percent, making sure Big would pay him whether or not the clonebot himself made money off record sales. DiMachio decided on a twenty-four percent royalty for the next international mega super rock star, on eighty-five percent, or approximately eighteen percent on one hundred percent, an extremely low royalty figure for any musician destined to the heights of fame that Big was. As a finishing touch to DiMachio's deal with Big, he made himself executor of Big's estate and sole heir to any future royalties, should anything happen to the clonebot. Deity

DiMachio also named Jeremy Wickett beneficiary of a two-million-dollar life insurance policy he had Acht Records take out on Big, though DiMachio buried the details within mountains of Big paperwork. DiMachio saw the insurance merely as insurance, a way to compensate himself should something unexpected happen.

As soon as Big learned how to sign his name on the dotted line of the contract, DiMachio began implementing the clonebot's development program. Phase One consisted of general education and manipulation tactics. A team of trained professionals, unaware of Big's true identity and thinking him only a foreigner from the jungles of Brazil, were hired to teach Big reading and writing. DiMachio and Jeremy Wickett had decided arithmetic might be too risky; a record company never wanted their artists to add up the numbers.

Big spent his earth simulated, though technically unnecessary, sleeping hours with headphones over his ears while recorded messages swam through his computerized brain. 'DiMachio knows all; DiMachio rules all; you will follow all DiMachio says' played all night long, in addition to 'Acht is your home; Acht is your family; Acht is your life.' DiMachio had ordered Big to listen to the Acht affirmations and brainwashing as an extra-added measure to ensure the clonebot's loyalty. The same messages were piped through the halls and offices of the record company monolith, though the sound frequency was so high human ears could not detect the messages, but the brain absorbed them.

DiMachio looked out his window and stared up Broadway, deep in thought. The consulting firm of Butler and Bua had just concluded an emergency, one hundred-thousand-dollar, intensive market research study on image and the rock star. Their findings mirrored the general consensus of his executive staff. Big's initial black leather, biker look was out of date. The music that went along with the look was also outdated and was considered merely a trend. Butler and Bua recommended a more middle-of-the-road approach, including a softer image and musical style for the clonebot. Big would have longer career potential if he emulated the singing style and image of such crooners as Neil Diamond, Frank Sinatra. or even Tony Bennett.

DiMachio slowly digested the consultant information with his right hand, Jeremy Wickett, and became comfortable with the idea of Big as the next international mega superstar balladeer rock singer.

The intercom buzzed.

DiMachio walked over to his desk and punched his speaker button. "Yeah," he yelled into his machine and out to his assistant, Heysannah.

"There's a call from the lab. Something urgent about the Big development project."

"What do they want?"

"They wouldn't say, they said it was a TerraYak and it was important."

DiMachio hated interruptions and began simmering. He hit the spot next to the blinking green light and turned back to stare out his window.

"Hello?" floated timidly over the speaker phone and out into the office.

"What is it? And don't tell me the training's not working," said DiMachio.

"No, no, no," the fearful voice said. "We have a minor glitch, and we thought you might have some ideas that could help us."

DiMachio continued staring out his window and up the avenue. "Ask one of my executives."

"We wanted to ask you first. We thought you might not want your staff to know."

DiMachio felt the steam rising within him. "I'm on my way." He continued staring up Broadway while his body churned with frustration and executive impatience. He tilted his head as he tried to read the digital display board atop the Mutual of New York building. Hundreds of light bulbs flashed the current temperature and time to anyone who looked up in its direction. He glanced at his watch, one twenty-three. He looked back out the window and was almost positive the clock read one nineteen. He glanced at his watch again, then back out into the city.

DiMachio turned around and hit his intercom button.

"Yes," came through the speaker.

"Get in here now!"

His twin Swedish assistants, the Doublemint Girls of Rock, came rushing through the door, pen and paper in hand.

DiMachio pointed to a spot next to him. "Over here."

His assistants immediately obliged.

"There," said DiMachio as he pointed toward the window.

Hosannah and Heysannah looked at the city of concrete, metal and glass spread out before them.

"Do you see it?"

The Doublemint Girls of Rock glanced quickly at each other.

"Jesus, how dumb are you two? Look at the clock!"

His assistants did as they were told.

Steam spilled from DiMachio's ears. "Damn it, can't you see? It's four minutes slow! It's been four minutes slow for weeks. And look at all those burned-out light bulbs! How can anyone even read the time?!"

The women looked at each other again, confusion written all over their faces.

"You're certainly right," said Heysannah.

"I know I'm right, damn it." The Deity turned and glared at his assistants. "It's driving me crazy! Get it fixed!"

"Excuse me?" asked Hosannah.

DiMachio raised his voice even louder and spoke with exaggerated slowness. "Get the clock fixed! Get the burned-out bulbs replaced! I want to see the correct time on that clock tomorrow morning!"

DiMachio stormed past his open-mouthed assistants and took the executive elevator up two floors to the Yakadan training and development laboratory on thirty-eight.

When Deity DiMachio threw open the laboratory doors, a screeching sound of unimaginable proportions accosted him. He put his hands over his ears and went toward the source of the noise. When he turned a corner, he saw Big standing on a small stage with five ear-plugged, laboratory-coated Yakadans and a full-bodied opera-looking diva surrounding him.

"It's no use," said the diva as she threw her fattened arms up in exasperation. "He is not teachable. He is not a singer. I can teach him no more."

"The hell he's not," DiMachio bellowed as he approached the group.

"Then you teach him to sing," said the music diva. She turned on her heel and disappeared from the room.

The TerraYak nervously cleared his throat. "Ah, Mr. DiMachio. Nice of you to come. We seem to have a small problem."

DiMachio glared at the Yakadans. "What is it?"

"Well, it seems Mr. Big cannot sing. We were able to program speech into the clonebot because of TerraYaks like myself, but we think Mr. Big sings the vocal equivalent of our planetary sonar music. The programmer in charge of inner-digital musical programming must have assumed our two planets had the same type of music."

A wisp of steam curled out from DiMachio's right ear. "What can you do about it?"

"Unfortunately, nothing," said the TerraYak. "He doesn't seem capable of carrying a tune. He's completely tone deaf, even when it comes to Yakadan sonar singing."

"So?" asked the Deity. "Get him a transposer and have him sing through it."

"What is a transposer?" asked the TerraYak.

"It's a machine that puts singers on key. As long as Big sings through a microphone, he'll be on key. We use it for some of our artists."

"We might have a slight problem with that," said the laboratory-coated alien. "We can train him to sing words like you earthlings do, but the words will be sung with sonar screeching sounds. And I doubt even your transposer machine will be able to correct the noise and make musical words."

Steam escaped DiMachio's ears and left nostril. "Can he lip synch?"

"I'm sorry, what is lip synch?" said the TerraYak.

The kettle began to boil. "Mouth the words. Can he pretend he's singing by mouthing the words, but no sound comes out of his mouth?"

"I'm not sure." The TerraYak turned to the clonebot. "Big, could you sing the song again, except this time don't let anything come out of your mouth. Just pretend you're singing."

Big nodded with his limited understanding. One of the laboratory coated Yakadans turned on the tape deck. "Tiny Dancer" floated out of the speakers and into the air. Big pretended to sing, his mouth moving to the words, yet no sound escaping.

"See," said DiMachio. "He could be Elton John for all anyone knew."

"What should we do?" asked the TerraYak.

"Milli Vanilli!" DiMachio screamed. "Hire some schlep, pay him a lot of money and threaten him with bodily harm so he keeps his mouth shut. Have him sing. All Big has to do when he performs is lip sync to prerecorded tracks that we'll pipe out through the sound system. It's been done before, and it can be done again." Deity DiMachio glared at the group of Yakadans. "And make damn sure you don't get caught."

As DiMachio walked away from the clonebot and gathering of aliens, he heard a nervous throat-clearing sound behind him. DiMachio stopped in his tracks. "What else is wrong with him?" he asked without turning around.

"Well, Mr. DiMachio, sir, Big's dance and rhythm teacher has mentioned that Big has a slight problem with his dance classes."

The Deity and Ruling Dictator turned around and faced the TerraYak. "Why are you things having so many problems? And why aren't you going to your Head Yak? I have a company to run!"

The TerraYak cleared his throat again. "The Head Yakadan told us we reported to you with regard to Mr. Big. He said you run the company and you know what you're doing when it comes to making music. He said his part of the project was positioning the clonebot within the company; your job is to get him out to the public."

"What's the machine's problem now?" said DiMachio impatiently.

"He can't dance well."

"What does that mean - he can't dance well? What is 'well'?"

"Umm, it seems Mr. Big has two left feet as you would say on this planet."

"Keep him seated on a stool or standing in one place in front of a microphone. No dancing, ever. If we feel the need to liven up his stage show, we'll hire professional dancers to bump and grind around him. But he always remains still. Understand?"

The TerraYak nodded silently. DiMachio left the room, nearly scalding himself with steam. "Damn aliens," he said to his trusted confidante, Jeremy Wickett, who had, as always, discreetly followed along with his master. He stormed back into his private executive elevator. "They said this was easy. We were guaranteed success. That clonebot thing is as much trouble as most of the artists on the label. With the same amount of talent!"

Jeremy nodded, though this time he was unable to appease his boss' pent up frustration.

Eight

On an uneventful Tuesday, no more uneventful than all the Tuesdays before, Alex rode the elevator to yet another interview. Langley never again mentioned the day he fired her, so Alex stayed at her job, too tired to care, too lost to know what to do.

Today's meeting was with Sturgeon Westfield, the young, hip, recently promoted Vice President of Post-Mortem Product Development taking the company by storm. As Alex walked toward his office, she saw him leaning against the doorway, his sunken eyes gazing blankly off into the distance. He was thin; he was wiry; he looked nearly emaciated as his black Armani suit and white T-shirt hung limply around him. His face was pale and waxen, and Alex thought she detected a little eye shadow and rouge applied ever so expertly.

As Alex reached Westfield's office, he extended a long delicate manicured hand in front of her. His handshake was limp, and Alex had the strangest feeling there was no life in the limb she was touching. Westfield's straight cut, below the ear, lifeless black hair stayed perfectly in place as he invited Alex into his office. As she walked through the doorway, a faint whiff of incense drifted into her nostrils. She heard soft organ music in the background as she sat in one of the cushioned high-backed armless guest chairs. The room was dimly lit, with wreaths of flowers resting on easels dotted around. In the center of the wreaths were eight and a half by eleven color glossies of dead Acht artists. A candle flickered silently in the far corner.

Post-Mortem Product Development was a new field, an area in which people created and implemented innovative, cutting-edge ways of bringing music from dead musicians to the public. Alex should have been excited over the prospect of working in such a department, a new area of the record company in which new territories could be explored, but nothing could penetrate the numbness that now followed her everywhere.

Westfield looked across his thick black desk with black vacant eyes. "How are you feeling today, Alex?" he asked in a concerned, hushed tone.

Alex shrugged her shoulders but remained silent.

Westfield leaned forward, his hollow stare like the glass eyes of a wax mannequin. "Any ailments, dizziness, anything dragging you down and making you feel tired?"

Alex tried to brush off the nagging feeling that had followed her to the interview. "No," she forced herself to say.

Westfield leaned a little closer. "You're sure?"

"Yes," said Alex with forced enthusiasm as her stomach cried out for something sweet.

Westfield sat back and let out a small sigh. "Very well," he said, his mouth turned down into a small frown.

He straightened his already straightened telephone, calculator, business card holder and box of tissues, making sure they were touching and in a straight line.

"So, Alex, who recommended you for the job?"

"Personnel."

Westfield continued in his quiet, hushed tone. "Ah, personnel, yes. A good group of people." Vice President of Post-Mortem Product Development Westfield glanced over Alex's resume, the only visible piece of paper in his office. "I can see you're qualified, but it's not all about qualifications." With a slow dramatic gesture fit for B-movie Hollywood, he waved his arms toward his kingdom of post-mortem product development, a kingdom contained within his office walls. "I need to find the right person who fits in, who'll get along with me. We'll be like a team, and I'm looking for someone who thinks like me and has my interests."

Alex nodded glumly.

Westfield looked solemnly at Alex. "Why do you want to leave your job?"

Alex took a deep breath and sighed. In a flat voice, she said, "I've worked for Langley for over two years and I've peaked as far as gaining knowledge and moving within the department…"

"Ah, yes, I understand," said Westfield interrupting, his eyes becoming more lifelike. "I was in the exact same situation earlier in my career. I come from marketing, you know. Spent time in the California and London offices but after five years, I felt I'd peaked. Fortunately, Derby knew of my good work, and that I worked in a funeral home to pay my way through college." Westfield let out a sigh and looked at the candle burning slowly in the corner. "That was a great job, very soothing, very peaceful." Westfield looked back at Alex, his dentally whitened teeth shining into a slow smile. "Derby decided I was perfect for the then new job in Post-Mortem Product Development." Westfield raised his waxen manicured hands. "And see how it worked out. There I was, a director of marketing and ex-funeral home expert, feeling unchallenged and ready to move on when, voila, I get this job."

Alex nodded silently, barely paying attention. Westfield probably had nothing to do, no meetings to go to, nothing, as he waited for rock stars to die.

She retained her interview etiquette and forced herself to focus on him, a smile of agreement plastered on her face. A vague thought popped into her mind but she pushed it away before it could take shape.

"So, Alex, any questions for me?"

She looked through the dim light at Westfield. "What exactly is post-mortem product development?"

Westfield slowly breathed in the incense-scented air. "After the death of Kirby Propane, senior management started post-mortem product development, or PMPD as I call it. Just think of the dead superstars – Cobain, Hutchinson, Lennon, and so on. I find ways to sell records from bands with at least one dead member." Westfield sat up straighter and pulled gently on his blazer lapels, smoothing out a stray wrinkle that had wandered into his clothing. "Think of it. Rock stars are aging, and they'll start dying soon. When they do, it's my job to make sure there are records to buy for decades to come."

Alex knew the silence was her cue. Feeling as enthusiastic as one of the corpses Westfield used to work on, she asked, "Can you tell me anything specific about your job?"

Westfield's arm slowly rose in another exaggerated gesture. "There are so many things, so many." His eyes looked off into the distance as he leaned forward. "Secrets, there are lots of secrets. We can't let other companies know what we're doing, but seeing as you

66

asked, I'll tell you one." Westfield looked sternly at Alex. "But only one. My assistant is the only one who knows the secrets, and she'll have her memory wiped clean when she leaves the job. No memory of ever working here." Westfield lowered his voice to almost a whisper. "It's better that way; no leaks."

Alex leaned forward and sarcastically whispered back, "If you don't want to tell me, that's fine."

Westfield smiled down at Alex. "No, no, it's alright. I like you, so I'll give you one, but you have to promise you won't tell."

Alex held up her right hand and rolled her eyes. "I promise."

"Okay." Westfield's eyes slowly scanned his office, resting briefly on the photos of the dead artists surrounding him. "You know how we released a couple of Kirby Propane records, even though he's dead?"

Alex nodded.

"What we did was feed everything we had on him into a computer. All his lyrics, all his music, all the words he ever spoke on TV and radio interviews, and so on. We created this computer program that could calculate the pitch of each of his words and his music. We pushed a few buttons, did a little tweaking, and got a couple more albums out of him."

Alex knew record companies were ruthless, but she was caught off guard at the depths Acht would sink to make more money. But she wasn't surprised. Corporations not only bred incompetence, she realized they were also powerhouses of greed and corruption. "Are you saying you took other stuff he'd done and made new songs from them?"

"Exactly." Westfield was beaming. "The miracle of computers."

Even though disgusted, Alex's interest was piqued. "But how…"

"Who cares?" said Westfield. "What's important is we got ourselves a couple more records, more money for us." He let out a small chuckle. "And, boy, did they sell. Millions of copies flying off store shelves, and people all thinking it was music we had stored in the vaults. I was ingenious."

Once again, Alex had an uncomfortable, nagging feeling, but she pushed it aside. She forced herself to speak.

"What exactly would my job be?"

Westfield folded his hands on his desk, looking alive for the first time since the interview began. "You would do what I need done. Period."

Another standardized question fell out of Alex's mouth. "Are you interviewing many people?"

"Ah," replied Westfield. His hushed mortician tone turned nervous. "Interviewing. Well, I'm interviewing a few people, here and there, people personnel are sending up, you know, just to see."

Alex shifted in her chair, the cushion suddenly not as comfortable as she first thought. "I'm sorry, to see what?"

"Just to see," said Westfield as he re-straightened the already straightened objects on his desk. "You know, if someone might be better than the person I've already chosen. He looked up at her and smiled a waxy mortician pseudo-smile. "I mean, I'm glad you're interested in the job, but I've already decided who I'm hiring."

"What am I doing here?" said Alex, realizing she was wasting her time.

"I didn't have a choice." Westfield glanced blankly toward Alex. "Personnel insisted I see a few people."

Alex had enough and stood. "Thank you for your time, it was a pleasure meeting you," she lied.

Westfield made no effort to shake her hand. As Alex turned away, she saw him fold her resume and drop it in the trash can beside his desk.

*

Exhausted, Alex walked on the elevator and punched thirty-five. All that time and energy wasted in a useless interview for a job she'd never get. As she looked up and watched the floor numbers increasing one by one, she had that nagging, frightening thought again. And this time it took shape. What if it wasn't just Westfield, or Langley, or even Acht? She pushed it away and reached into her pocket. She pulled out her current favorite, a snack-sized Snickers bar, and shoved the candy into her mouth. With each chew, she felt a little better.

When the doors opened on thirty-five, she walked off the elevator, her eyes reflexively squinting from the stark blinding glare of the overhead fluorescent lights. "Kung Fu Fighting" filled the air as

Hellie sat stationed at her desk, her Ticonderoga number two pencil tapping lightly against the aquarium glass. Her mutant sea creatures performed their synchronized underwater dance routine.

Hellie put down her pencil and turned off the music. "What's wrong?"

"The usual," said Alex, pulling out another piece of candy from her pocket. "I just went to an interview and was told the job was already filled." She bit the mini chocolate bar in half. Through her chewing, she said, "I'm so tired of all this."

"I'm sorry," said Hellie as she quietly dipped her hand into her aquarium and gently caressed her mutant sea creatures.

As Alex looked at Hellie's desk, something seemed wrong; something definitely seemed missing.

Alex gasped. "Oh my god," she said with genuine shock as she took a small step back and stared at Hellie. "Your cerebrum urn is missing. What did you do?"

Hellie replied nonchalantly, "I told the Cerebrum Security Patrol I was getting migraines from the fluorescent lights, so I asked for a smoked black urn. Sort of sunglasses for my brain."

Alex completely forgot about her interview. "And they're letting you keep your brain in until it arrives?"

Hellie shrugged her shoulders. "Yes, but the urn came yesterday."

Alex's eyes widened. "Where is it?"

"In my drawer." Hellie grinned mischievously. "Want to see something even better?"

Alex nodded, unable to believe Hellie's blatant disregard for the rules. She shoved the rest of the candy in her mouth and licked the melting chocolate off her fingers.

Hellie looked around, making sure no one was in the immediate vicinity. She motioned for Alex to come to her side of the desk. Hellie pulled open the bottom drawer and pulled out a package wrapped in brown paper. Behind the package was her sparkling new urn, complete with fresh, semi-pasteurized brain nutrient juice. She picked up the urn and placed it on the floor between her feet. Hellie then carefully untied the string from the wrapped package, saving it for possible later use, and removed the paper. Alex put her hand to her mouth and gasped again. There, inside the paper, resting on Hellie's lap, was a brain.

"It's rubber," said Hellie matter-of-factly as she picked up the cerebrum and dropped it into her new urn. She carefully lifted the black-tinted container and placed it on her desk in the proper cerebrum place.

Alex was stunned. "How on earth?"

"Gift store."

"What?" exclaimed Alex.

Hellie's grin broke into a large smile. "The card and gift store just down the block."

Alex was reeling. "But why would they have brains?"

Hellie shrugged. "Guess I'm not the first to come up with the idea."

"But aren't you afraid?"

Hellie smiled. "Of what, of them finding out? So what? All they can do is fire me."

"But doesn't that scare you?"

"Of course not. I can always find work somewhere."

Alex looked at Hellie. "I don't understand you. I put up with this because I want to work in music. And I know Langley would never give me a good reference if I quit, so I put up with all this. But if you're sure you can get another job, why do you stay here?"

Hellie shrugged matter-of-factly. This pays more than working in a hamburger joint, so I'm content to sit here for a few years while I work toward getting what I really want. And because this is part of the journey toward my goal, it's okay. It doesn't bother me. It's simply part of the process."

Alex was confused. "What in the world are you talking about?"

Hellie smiled. "The fun isn't the goal; the fun is everything you do to get to that goal."

Alex rolled her eyes in exasperation.

"Hi guys."

Alex and Hellie looked over and saw Zena, clad in her now-usual lingerie and six-inch heels, as she sashayed up to the reception desk.

"Hi," they both replied under-enthusiastically.

"What are you doing?"

"Talking," said Alex.

"About what?" asked Zena with wide-eyed innocence and bushy-tailed curiosity.

"The usual," said Alex semi-sarcastically. "Why no one will hire me."

Zena giggled. "Oh, I know why, so don't worry about it."

Alex looked at Zena. She had a feeling her day had just gotten worse. "What do you mean, Zena?"

Zena spoke in her sugar sweet, candy-coated voice. "Langley was in my Jiglio's office a while ago, and I heard them talking. Someone in the promotion department called Jiglio to see about hiring you. Jiglio asked Langley about you, and Langley said something about you being okay at what you do but you don't understand your place in the company, that you're here to wait on him, and you don't do it with the right attitude."

Alex and Hellie looked at each other.

"Later, I told Jiglio you were a good person and everyone liked you, but he said he couldn't take you away from Langley because Langley's a troublemaker and had such a hard time finding someone that lasted more than six weeks. He was afraid if he took you away Langley would go crazy and take it out on the promotion department. So, everyone's afraid to hire you because they're all scared of Langley." Zena flipped back her purple rinsed black hair. "So, you see, it's not as bad as you think." The brainless assistant smiled from ear to ear.

"Fuck," was all that escaped from Alex's mouth.

Alex turned on her heel and headed back to her desk. She pulled a Kit Kat out of her sweater pocket and ripped it open. As she finished the first piece, she saw Skeater walking toward her with his stuffed ferret, Skat, snuggled under his arm. Alex shoved the rest of the candy into her mouth and looked down quickly, trying to chew. She glanced sideways and saw a stuffed ferret with sunglasses glide by her field of vision.

"Hi," said Skeater from behind his Starsky sunglasses as he passed her.

Alex looked up quickly, her hair black and purple, her face flushed. "Hi," came out in a muffled baritone as she tried to finish the candy. She felt melting chocolate and saliva drip out of the side of her mouth. She hurried the last few yards to her secretarial suite. She rushed around her desk and yanked down her skull zipper with such force she nearly toppled herself over. She pulled out her brain and threw it in her Acht cerebrum urn, paying no attention to the nutrient juice that splashed over herself and her desk. Alex rezipped and fell into her chair, panting heavily, her breath the smell of overly sweet chocolate.

*

Skeater turned and watched Alex rush away. He knew nothing about her, except she had the most beautiful hair he'd ever seen, and he had this strange feeling whenever he was around her that he'd known her all his life.

Skeater started back toward Langley's office, then stopped. What was he doing? The screaming startled Skeater. He looked around him and realized he had somehow wandered into Langley's outer office. Alex's cerebrum urn was sitting on her desk. Though he knew it was impossible, her brain looked thoroughly depressed as it drooped aimlessly in its nutrient juice. Skeater looked closer at the urn. He could have sworn Alex's brain had just let out the most depressing sigh ever. He never understood the cerebrum extraction procedure, he had been one of the few executives who had fought the company to try to change the policy, but he never begrudged the employees who put themselves through it.

He couldn't see anyone, but he recognized the voices.

"Where in the hell have you been?!"

"I was at lunch and then I went to the bathroom."

"I don't want excuses; I want you at your desk! This note is urgent. Deliver it immediately!"

Alex walked out of Langley's office with her head down. She jumped back with fright as she nearly knocked Skeater over. Her face burned as beads of perspiration popped out all over her body. Trembling, she looked at him.

"He, he's in there if you need him," she said. "Just go in."

Alex rushed by Skeater, her hair streaming blue behind her, and raced to photocopy and deliver the urgent note to one of the ten vice presidents of law, a note that read, "Status of Campbell renegotiation? Call me to discuss."

Skeater sighed and watched Alex disappear out the door. He tightened his grip around Skat and walked down the hall to the elevator, feeling deflated and empty.

Nine

One morning, DiMachio had an idea.

"Heysannah, get my executive staff in here now!" he said into his intercom. Deity DiMachio sat on his fur lined gilt trimmed leather throne and stared out his window, watching the minutes pass by accurately on the digital clock atop the skyscraper in his city landscape field of vision.

Within minutes, he heard a sharp knock. He looked over in the direction of the sound and electronically opened the richly stained, antique mahogany door halfway down his football-field-sized office. His executive staff stumbled in and quickly took their places around the executive conference room table at the far end of the room.

Hosannah appeared in the electrically motorized Acht transmobile and chauffeured the Deity down the red carpeted path to where his executives awaited. He stepped out of the golf cart and settled in his throne, Jeremy Wicket, swollen with excitement and anticipation, one step in front of him.

He glared from executive to executive. "I have an idea."

His staff gave him their full attention. Deities usually heard other people's ideas; rarely did they have their own. Skeater tugged on his ear and turned off his music.

DiMachio stared at the executives, his satanic eyes daring any of them to challenge the plan he had formulated only minutes earlier in his office. "Big. I've been thinking about his development program. It's taking too long. Has he started recording yet?"

"A few weeks ago," said Skeater as he casually petted Skat.

Unknown to Skeater or any other Senior Senior Executive President, Big wasn't actually recording. DiMachio had ordered Big to go to the studio every day and sing into a turned off microphone; a hired session singer, sworn to the utmost secrecy with bribes and death threats, and a lot of money, lent his voice as Big's. Big, with his I.Q. of 80, was unaware he couldn't sing and had no idea someone else was recording the songs.

DiMachio smirked. "How many songs are recorded so far?"

Senior Senior Executive President of A&R Skeater adjusted his Starsky racing shades. "Two, if I'm not mistaken."

"How long to finish another song?"

"He's taking a week or two for each song."

"I want five songs recorded, mixed and mastered by the end of next week," said DiMachio.

"What?" asked Skeater. "But there's mixing and mastering and..."

DiMachio's reptilian face seethed with anger. "I don't give a shit what there is; I want five songs finished by the end of next week."

Jiglio's steely black eyes looked at his boss and the overall Ruling Dictator of the record company. "That's impossible."

"Bullshit," said DiMachio as the familiar anger steam began escaping his ears. "Have them work twenty-four hours a day if you have to, but I want five songs in a week and a half."

Senior Senior Executive President of Promotion Jiglio narrowed his eyes. "But if we have more time..."

"We don't have more time," said Deity and Ruling Dictator DiMachio. "Not only am I executive producer of Big's records, I'm also Deity of this company."

DiMachio saw the ice harden in Jiglio's eyes, felt the resentment and hatred boiling up in his subordinate, but he knew he would be met with silence. Lines of authority had to be obeyed in every company, without exception, and no one dared talk back or argue with him. If they did, they knew the consequences.

Deity DiMachio continued, satisfied he now had everyone's full attention. "I want a five-song CD to introduce Big while we wait for his full-length album. Derby, how fast can we do it?"

Derby stared at the ceiling.

DiMachio looked at Derby with disgust. "This isn't fucking brain surgery, Derby. Just give me a time."

Derby jumped, his ornate silver fork clattering to the table. "Umm, I'd say two months."

"Two fucking months to get a lousy CD5 out?" exclaimed DiMachio in disbelief. "What in the hell takes so long?"

"He's right," said Jiglio, pointing toward Derby. "It's a week or two to finish the songs, six weeks for the plant to put the record together, and a couple days for shipping, delays, that sort of thing."

"I want this record out and number one in two months," said DiMachio.

"Impossible," replied Jiglio. "I need more than a month to get it going at radio. And I need music before I start promoting it."

Deity DiMachio leaned forward in his fur lined gilt trimmed leather throne, steam shooting from every orifice. "I don't give a fuck what you need. I want a number one record, and I want it now." He looked at each of his executives. "You assholes work for me. I want something, I get it. I don't get it; you get another job. Everyone here got that?"

*

Jiglio looked at his boss poker faced. No one treated him that way, not even DiMachio. He was the best promotion person in the business, any label would hire him, and probably for more money than DiMachio was paying him. He could go anywhere. Jiglio suddenly had a better idea. Why should he have to go anywhere? Why should he have to uproot himself and go to another company. Yes, there were other options…

"JIGLIO, are you listening to me?!"

Jiglio looked evenly at DiMachio, his sheet of ice betraying nothing. "Of course, DiMachio."

"Then answer me!"

"Answer what?"

"How long to get to number one?"

"Depends. With enough money, we might be able to release the record at number one. But we need set up time."

DiMachio pounded his fists on the arms of his throne. "Four months, that's it. I want a huge party for Big in four months. That gives you two months to get the damn thing out and two months to get it to number one." DiMachio glared around the table. "And he better be the most famous singer in the world by then."

Weena popped her Xanax like candy. "What kind of party do you want?"

DiMachio looked at her with disgust. "Do you have a brain?! What do I pay you for?"

Weena nodded as parts of her body randomly fell on the conference room table.

"Big! I want the biggest party this company has ever seen. I want everyone invited. I want everyone in this business to know who Big is, and who's responsible for him."

Weena hastily scribbled on her notepad as she discreetly tried to round up her body parts.

DiMachio looked over his staff. "You people disgust me. I don't know how this company makes money."

He pushed a button under the conference room table and returned to his Acht transmobile. Heysannah rushed in and drove him back to his desk.

*

The next morning the executive staff was in an uproar as they gathered in the smaller, thirty-fifth floor conference room to discuss Big.

"Let's get started," Jiglio announced.

The executives all took a seat and looked at the promotion executive.

Jiglio held up a stack of papers that had been in front of him. "I say we do the Fast Track Superstar Plan."

Derby, Langley and Weena nodded and each held up a thick pile of their own papers.

Jiglio pushed back his chair and stood up. "Fast Track Superstar Plan it is then. Let's have our people do some real work for a change." He smirked and walked out of the conference room.

Skeater simply shook his head.

*

Jiglio returned to his office and paced the length of his eight hundred square foot room. It was boring, the same thing day in and day out. He'd peaked in his position as Senior Senior Executive President of Promotion, and there was only one step left to take, one more promotion that would bring him to the pinnacle of his career, and that step was on to Vinny DiMachio's throne.

Jiglio continued to pace up and down, past his black leather and chrome steel couch and chrome and glass coffee table, past his black marble desk, to the far side of his office. He stopped and stared at his naked steel blue, non-regulation wall, his mind conjuring up corporate sabotage and takeover options. The Expense Audit Embezzlement Scheme wouldn't work. The Yakadans wouldn't care how much DiMachio stole from the company unless they wanted to get rid of him. The Massive Monetary Pay-Off Scheme wouldn't work either unless there was a reason to let DiMachio go. A company wouldn't pay an executive millions of dollars to leave unless there was a good reason to get them out.

The Promotion man was left with two options, the Accidental Death or Dismemberment Procedure or the Gross Negligence and Incompetence Scheme. Even though Jiglio was partial to the Accidental Death Procedure, he knew if DiMachio died, whether by a random drive-by shooting or a slow painful poisoning, the Family would investigate. And for all the power, control and ultimate domination Jiglio believed he deserved, he would never jeopardize his relationship with the Family, and he would never instigate the death of one of its members. It would mean his own death.

Jiglio turned away from the wall and slowly paced back across his office. The last viable option he had was the Gross Negligence and Incompetence Scheme. This strategy was the most difficult to implement, largely because most employees in the music industry were grossly incompetent to begin with, and they made money for the company despite themselves.

Jiglio slowed his steps until he stopped in the middle of his office, his icy eyes unfocussed, his corrupt mind processing possibilities. He snapped his fingers as a slow, evil smirk spread across his face. Jiglio rushed over to his desk and sat down, flipping through his Rolodex. He picked up the phone, but before he put it to his ear he sat back and stared at the receiver, wondering if the equipment was bugged. He knew he couldn't take any chances; DiMachio wasn't Deity and Ruling Dictator by sheer luck. Jiglio placed the receiver back in the cradle and jotted down a number from his personal Rolodex. He slipped the piece of paper into his blue pinstripe blazer pocket and left his office without a word of his intended whereabouts to Zena. Senior Senior Executive President of Promotion Jiglio stepped onto the private executive elevator and descended to the ground floor.

There was only one thing important enough to the Yakadans to hold DiMachio fully responsible. There was only one thing that could happen to make DiMachio lose his job, and Jiglio knew what it was. The Promotion man icily smirked as he formulated his corporate sabotage plan. First, motive had to be contrived, laid out and framed. Then execution of the Gross Negligence and Incompetence Master Plan would be put into place.

Jiglio stepped off the executive elevator and walked through Checkpoint Vinny without a glance from the armed security officers. He left the building, congratulating himself on his devious astuteness and malicious deductive reasoning, important characteristics for any top record executive, and essential attributes necessary to implement his plan. As he walked across the street and up the avenue, he jotted down inerasable and undetectable mental notes. There were details to take care of, seeds of destruction to be planted, preparations to be made.

Too paranoid to use his cell phone, Jiglio stopped at a payphone three blocks from the corporate monolith. He dropped money into the slot and dialed the number he had jotted down in his office. After two rings, a female voice answered.

"Jiglio here. Get me Bret Horowitz."

Ten

The staff of Acht worked around the clock to finish Big's record and release him to the public. As DiMachio had ordered, Big's short-length CD *Love, Love, Lovin' You* was released on the day the Deity and Ruling Dictator had ordered. A month and millions of dollars later Big became, well, Big. Bigger than the Beatles could have hoped to be, bigger than Bruce Springsteen. Big was even bigger than rock star Barbie.

The planet became infested with Big memorabilia, from Big dolls and Big guitars to Big clothes including Big suits, ties, and swim trunks, as well as Big calendars, watches, coffee mugs, key chains, jewelry, Big personal hygiene products, greeting cards, wrapping paper, and board games. New Big products were created every day. There were even a Big cartoon and Big game show in production, where, naturally, everything was bigger than life. Big was feted and wooed, talked about and admired in almost every household in America, and many around the world.

Deity DiMachio had approved a budget of over twenty million dollars for the marketing and promotion of *Love, Love, Lovin' You* in the U.S. alone. It didn't matter that other label artists suffered from lack of money for their records; Big was a priority. And he was everywhere.

His handsomely exotic face appeared overnight on billboards around the country as well as in nationally distributed magazines and newspapers. His video for "Love", one of the songs off his record, aired nonstop on TV music channels. His songs were played on Top 40, adult contemporary, classic rock, adult album alternative, and album-oriented rock radio, a crossover hit of such magnitude the country exploded Big.

DiMachio put down his latest copy of Soundscan, the national charting system that tracked records sold, and smirked. Perhaps his staff had actually done something right this time. Big had already sold five million units in the U.S. alone, and sales projections were exponentially positive.

Deity DiMachio reached over and congratulated his confidante, Jeremy Wickett, for their combined success. At five million units and rapidly rising, DiMachio knew his three percent producer royalty would make him richer than he already was. He had structured Big's contract so he was paid his three percent off retail sales figures, with no regard to recoupability issues.

Big, on the other hand, would have all relevant costs and expenses deducted from his royalty figures before he would see a penny. Big had to repay the company the advance they gave him to live off, the recording costs associated with making his record, as well as a percentage of the money paid out by the record company for various marketing, promotion, and publicity expenses. Even with millions of CD5's already sold, DiMachio doubted Big had earned a dollar yet, due to his enormous contractual recoupable costs.

DiMachio pressed his intercom. "One of you get in here," he barked into the machine.

Hosannah immediately appeared at his desk.

Deity DiMachio handed her a videocassette. "Put it in."

Hosannah turned on his television equipment and popped the tape into the machine. She pressed play and adjusted the volume to DiMachio's standard audio specifications.

"Leave."

Hosannah placed the remote-control unit on DiMachio's desk and left the room.

DiMachio leaned back comfortably in his throne and stared at his six-foot television screen. He didn't normally take much interest in the details of any of his artists, but Big was different. DiMachio had a lot of money to make off the alien machine.

Applause roared through his Dolby surround sound system, not aimed directly at him, but his nonetheless. A feeling of contentment and almost joy spread through Deity and Ruling Dictator DiMachio's body.

"Heysannah," he bellowed into his intercom.

"Yes, Deity DiMachio."

"Get me a thirty-minute tape of cheering and hysterical applause, out of control stuff. I want it blaring in my office every morning when I get here."

There was a pause on the other end.

"Heysannah, did you hear me?!"

"Uh, yes, Deity DiMachio."

DiMachio clicked off and turned his attention back to the Winona Brisbane show.

Winona Brisbane, the most popular daytime TV talk show host, stood in front of the camera, her perfectly tailored lavender mini skirt and blazer accenting her year-round deep olive skin and long tanned-looking legs. Her hair and makeup were perfect, her nose was perfect, everything about her was so flawless she almost seemed unreal, like she herself was part robot or clone. She held the microphone up toward her mouth.

"You ain't gonna believe this, ladies and gentlemen, but my surprise guest today is the most popular man on the planet."

A collective gasp and several hopeful screeches came from the audience. DiMachio rolled his eyes.

"We don't know how we got him here, but everyone give a big round of applause to music's biggest superstar, Big!"

The camera quickly panned the audience as people leapt to their feet screaming and cheering. Women trembled, cried, and several fainted. The camera zoomed back to the stage as Big ambled out in a hand stitched, custom-made designer suit.

His hair was perfectly styled and his makeup was subtle, yet effective. With his seven-foot towering height, he could have been a celestial god. The screams grew louder. Winona visibly shook as Big walked across the stage toward her. Big had perfected the second most charming smile DiMachio had ever seen; DiMachio's was better. The Deity laughed aloud as Big tripped over his own two enormously big clumsy feet. He regained his balance and gave a wave to the audience, who in turn screamed and cheered even louder.

"Stupid morons," DiMachio yelled at the television. "He's a bumbling idiot!"

Big leaned down and gave Winona a small peck on the cheek. Winona's knees buckled and she fell into her chair, fanning herself. The studio was in an uproar, the noise deafening. Big sat down next to

Winona. The crowd yelled even louder. Big took a sip of water. The crowd went crazier.

Winona held her hands in the air and yelled something to the audience, but nothing could be heard over the screaming. She got up from her chair and went to the edge of the crowd, putting her fingers to her lips.

The crowd calmed down enough for Winona to speak. "We aren't going to have any time for the interview if you all don't take your seats and quiet down."

The camera shot to Big. The clonebot was sitting in his chair, a blank expression on his face, as if he didn't know where he was. He stared upward toward the ceiling lights in the studio.

DiMachio shook his head. "He *looks* like a fucking moron. Why do all those women want him?" The Deity grunted.

Winona sat back next to Big. The audience calmed down to an almost controllable level. "Good afternoon, Big," Winona said in her seductively sweet alto voice.

"Hello, Winona," came the low and raspy reply.

If the room had gone crazy before, it was now in sheer pandemonium. Screaming pierced the air and was so uncontrollable the show broke to a commercial.

DiMachio pressed his intercom. Hosannah rushed in and fast-forwarded the tape through the commercials.

The show came back on. Winona had regained control.

"Big, will you sing for us today?"

Screeching sounds came from the audience but were quickly subdued.

"Sorry, Winona," said Big in his low, sexy voice as he uncrossed his legs. "I'm not singing live until my official pre-record release party."

A unified and saddened "Ohhhh" echoed throughout the room.

"Sorry, everyone," said Big to the audience.

Winona tucked her perfectly cut and sprayed, bottle black hair behind her ear. Her brown eyes were trained on Big. "Why, if I may ask?"

Big smiled a little smile, a kind of sympathy smile. DiMachio gave a grunt of satisfaction toward the grooming and etiquette teacher. The trainer had done the impossible, made a dumb piece of machinery practically presentable.

"Well, Winona, it's a record company thing. We thought it would be more exciting if we waited until my party, to help build the anticipation."

"Well, you're certainly doing that," said Winona as she batted her eyelashes.

"Christ, she's all over him," exclaimed DiMachio to the screen. "Is she blind?"

"But can't you do something special for us today, something we can remember?"

"Well, Winona, what do you have in mind?" asked Big as he stood up and took off his blazer.

The room erupted one more time. Big turned to the audience and held out his arms. He then closed them and embraced himself, as if to say he was embracing their love.

The crowd screamed even louder. Winona remained in her chair and looked Big up and down. Her eyes were filled with primitive animal lust. When Big put his hand up to the neck of his shirt and unbuttoned a button, it was all over. Women began racing toward the stage. Big unbuttoned a second button and the two women nearest him fainted.

"What a load of crap!" DiMachio bellowed. He hit his intercom. "Get in here now!"

Hosannah was in the room before he got out the last word.

"Get it out of my sight!" said DiMachio as he pointed to the TV screen.

Hosannah rushed over to the video player and ejected the tape. She turned off the equipment and disappeared.

DiMachio looked around his desk, agitated and angry. He hated watching his musicians anywhere. He even hated being out in public with them, unless it was at an industry function where people knew who really had the fame and power. They were nothing without him, absolutely nothing. He reached over and grabbed his favorite stack of files, his surveillance and blackmail files. That would make him feel better.

DiMachio had over fifty files on various Acht executives who were only a rung or two below him, his peers who ruled other record companies, anyone who was promoting rapidly through the conglomeration and who might become an eventual threat, as well as anyone Deity and Ruling Dictator DiMachio didn't like or trust.

He tossed aside several files and opened the folder on his most recent victim, Jiglio. DiMachio flipped through several shots of Jiglio having dinner with some shady looking characters in a popular Italian restaurant in Brooklyn, but he recognized them as Jiglio's brothers and cousins, and found nothing odd about guns on the table and money stacked next to the Senior Senior Executive President of Promotion. DiMachio grunted with dissatisfaction as he scrutinized the entire contents of Jiglio's file. The surveillance information only pointed to the usual Family activity.

As DiMachio closed the file, his eye caught one of the photos of Jiglio and his relatives having dinner. He pulled out the picture and studied it, this time noticing that one of the dinner guests was holding a photograph, though DiMachio could only see the white back of the picture. He knew the Family was sworn not to betray each other and assumed the dinner meeting was one of many the relatives had when they were discussing a new contract.

DiMachio glanced again at the white backside of the picture, unaware that the photo was a snapshot of Big.

DiMachio was interrupted by the sound of his intercom. He pressed the button on his speaker phone. "What!" he barked into the machine.

"Someone in the lobby is claiming to be Big's lawyer. He's demanding a meeting with you immediately."

"Get rid of him," said DiMachio.

"Security's tried, but he has signed documents and won't leave."

DiMachio trusted his instincts, and at that moment they were telling him that someone, somewhere, had fucked up.

"Send the asshole up," he said just before slamming his hand down on the phone, disengaging the speaker.

Within minutes there was a light knock on his door, followed by a brief appearance by Heysannah. "Your guest has arrived." His assistant disappeared as quickly as she had come.

DiMachio looked up and saw a large black leather briefcase with the engraved initials BH and pick proof, industrial strength, combination security locks suspended in midair. Steam escaped his ears as he realized something had gone wrong with their plan. Something foreign, something unforeseen, something despicable, unethical and relentless had slimed its way into his office.

It was Bret Horowitz, entertainment lawyer, one of the most powerful figures in the music business and certainly one of the most feared. He represented some of the biggest names in music, from superstar musicians and bands to producers and songwriters, as well as other ultra-famous entertainers and music industry moguls. He had his own law firm, Horowitz, Gillett, Goss, and Gardner, with twelve partners and over forty lawyers working for him. He was ruthless and would stop at nothing short of grossly illegal to get what he wanted.

DiMachio leaned back in his throne and watched as the black leather briefcase hung suspended in midair and slowly edged its way toward him. The Deity had to smirk over the twisted irony of what stood before him. Bret Horowitz, entertainment lawyer, had not only found a way to represent Big, DiMachio's most valuable and important artist, the lawyer was also DiMachio's personal business lawyer. Bret Horowitz, e.l., was under contract with Deity DiMachio to negotiate DiMachio's business dealings with Acht and to represent him on all miscellaneous legal business matters. Conflict of interest? Not in the music industry, a field where the few not only rule but also make up the rules.

The two-dimensional entertainment lawyer turned toward DiMachio, his fat, balding head and short stumpy body becoming visible.

"I was just admiring your gold and platinum record collection," said Bret Horowitz, e.l., as he pointed to the wall. "Nice to see so many of them are my clients."

With lightning speed, Horowitz reached into his inside pocket and pulled out his box of smiles, rapidly throwing on his proud, fatherly smile. He held out his hairy hand.

DiMachio returned the gesture and shook hands with his biggest business adversary, his legal counselor, and sometimes his personal friend. Deity DiMachio motioned to the guest chair across from his black marble desk and pushed his fresh ground and brewed coffee buzzer as he sat down.

DiMachio understood where the lines were drawn. Bret Horowitz, entertainment lawyer, might be ruthless in representing DiMachio, but he would be equally as ruthless in representing Big. Two-dimensional entertainment lawyers had only two loyalties, to themselves and to stuffing their bank accounts with as much cash as humanly possible, no matter where it came from. And at over five hundred dollars an hour, Horowitz had already filled a bank or two.

DiMachio leaned back in his throne and waited until Heysannah had poured them each a cup of his own special blend of Colombian and Venezuelan coffee, percolated but not boiled, and served in preheated china cups.

"I should have known it was you," said DiMachio with subtle malice as Heysannah disappeared from the room.

Bret Horowitz, e.l., took a sip of coffee, his smile returned to its box, the tight line that acted as his lips cutting across his face once again. He had a smile for every occasion and every mood in his treasured box of manufactured joy, but none remained on his face, none were real.

DiMachio took a satisfying sip of his coffee. "I guess I can assume you're not here to discuss my employment contract, now, are you?"

Bret Horowitz, e.l., quickly reached into his box of smiles and threw on a short chuckle. "Not today, my dear DiMachio. It seems I have a new client; someone I think you might know." The lawyer paused, the chuckle returned to its box, the silence calculated for effect.

DiMachio's intercom sounded. He slammed on the button. "What?" he growled.

"Deity DiMachio, Harvey Gildsteen is out here claiming to be Big's manager."

"Tell him I'm in a meeting," he said through gritted teeth.

Bret Horowitz, entertainment lawyer, put on his satisfied sucker smile. "Oh, actually, I invited him to join us."

DiMachio clenched the armrests on both sides of his throne. "You did what?!"

"I invited him to join us," said the entertainment lawyer smugly, the same smile still plastered into place.

Venom slid uncontrollably out of DiMachio's mouth. He hit the intercom. "Send him in."

Fat, unwashed, unkempt Harvey Gildsteen bounded joyfully into the office, his pleasantries as phony as the hair plugs dotted across the top of his round, roly-poly head.

"DiMachio, great to see you." Gildsteen shook hands with the Deity. "And, Bret, always a pleasure."

The manager and lawyer shook hands.

DiMachio was beside himself. Harvey Gildsteen, the stout, smooth-talking, rat-assed, anything-to-get-stinking-rich goon, was one of the most powerful managers in the music business. And now he too had a piece of Big.

"Where were we?" asked Bret Horowitz, e.l. "Right. We were discussing my new client."

"Our new client," said Gildsteen.

"Yes," said the entertainment lawyer. "Our new client...Big."

"How did you get to him?" said DiMachio as venom continued to drip from the side of his mouth.

The entertainment lawyer briefly whipped out another smile, this time the don't-ask-me-it's-a-professional-secret-but-I-sympathize smile. "It's my job," he said through his plastered-on smirk.

"We already have him under contract. He doesn't need a lawyer," said DiMachio.

Bret Horowitz, e.l., looked at Harvey Gildsteen and couldn't resist slapping on his we-all-know-I've-won-but-I-won't-rub-it-in-too

much smile. "Big had no legal representation, and he wasn't given fair counsel. Your contract would be thrown out the window of any courthouse."

Gildsteen nodded.

"What do you want?" asked DiMachio curtly, knowing civility would not make a difference.

"First," said the entertainment lawyer. "We both want our own copy of his contract." Bret Horowitz, e.l., unlocked his briefcase and pulled out a letter. He tossed it on the desk in front of DiMachio. Gildsteen followed suit. "Acceptance letters, fully notarized with Big's signature, stating we're representing him."

DiMachio punched his intercom.

"Yes, Deity DiMachio," came over the phone.

"Get Horowitz and Gildsteen copies of Big's contract," said DiMachio. He cut off the connection and glared at Bret Horowitz, entertainment lawyer. "What else?"

"Nothing right now," said the lawyer, clicking shut his briefcase and standing up. "I think we know what's next." He held out his hand, his I-beat-your-ass-sucker smile plastered on his face.

Gildsteen followed suit.

DiMachio returned the handshakes but said nothing. He watched Bret Horowitz, e.l., and Harvey Gildsteen leave his office, knowing full well what would come next.

As soon as Horowitz and Gildsteen received copies of Big's contract and left DiMachio's front office, DiMachio opened his mouth and erupted with a steam geyser that slammed his door shut. He ignored the sound of shattering glass as several of his framed platinum and gold records fell off his wall and crashed to the floor. He walked behind his desk and punched his telephone once again.

"Yes, Deity DiMachio," came over the speaker in war weary monotone.

"Except for Skeater, get that stupid-ass excuse of an executive team in here NOW!" DiMachio screamed. "And bring me the artist roster!"

"You might think you've won, you scum," DiMachio bellowed to the closed door and empty room. "All you mongrel-assed music peons who suck off and represent my artists might think you can get one over on me. But the game isn't over yet."

DiMachio leaned back in his throne, venom dripping from the side of his mouth. If Horowitz and Gildsteen wanted to play hardball, fine.

Heysannah came and disappeared before he knew she was in the room, but the roster appeared in front of him on his desk. DiMachio picked up his pen and thumbed through the pages.

"I think it's time for some roster rearranging," said DiMachio as he began earmarking musicians represented by Bret Horowitz, e.l., and Harvey Gildsteen. "I'll show them who has the most power; I'll show them all," he said, his mood returning to its normal malevolent state.

DiMachio heard a light tap and looked up to see the door silently opening. He stared at the space that had just been created and waited for someone to enter. When no one appeared, he felt his irritation begin to boil again.

"Whoever opened the door better get the hell in here, and get in here now," he said, a fresh ooze of venom sliding down from the side of his mouth toward his jaw.

He heard muffled scurrying sounds and whispering voices arguing outside in the front reception office. DiMachio knew his team had arrived. "Langley, Derby, Weena, and Jiglio, get the HELL in here now!!"

Jiglio entered first, his steps conveying authority and confidence, but the large red festering boil on his forehead betraying his apprehension. Langley followed in Jiglio's shadow, his body veiled in a cloud of cigarette smoke as he furiously puffed on three Winstons at the same time.

Weena stumbled into the office as if she had been pushed from behind, her right hand frantically keeping her left arm in place, her right eye swinging from her eye socket just below her chin while coils of her black Brillo-pad hair left a trail on the carpet. Derby brought up the rear, his sweaty, almost-bald head even shinier than usual, his gastrointestinal juices banging to the beat of their own drum.

DiMachio pointed across the football-field-sized room to his conference room table that seated nine. "Sit," he said with such force that the four executives leapt across the room and grabbed the first seat they could find. DiMachio hit his transportation buzzer and was quickly chauffeured in his electrically motorized Acht transmobile to his jewel encrusted throne at the head of the table.

"Where's Jeremy?" asked Weena as she desperately tried to glue herself back together.

"He's been excused from this meeting," said DiMachio in a venomous tone as he leaned forward. "He's too important for me to risk losing." He pointed a craggy finger in their direction. "But the rest of you are a different story."

DiMachio watched the four executives recoil, knowing his words had the intended impact. "Does anyone know what's going on with Big?"

Weena spoke up, her hands reglued and body parts bandaged, her nasal voice even more shaky than usual. "Well, Deity DiMachio, we have everything in place. His record's been favorably reviewed in every major magazine and newspaper in the country; he's given over a hundred interviews, has appeared on every major talk show."

"And," added Derby. "His CD-5 just passed sales of five and a half million units in the U.S. alone, and orders keep coming in."

"Every radio station is playing him," said Jiglio in a clipped, business-like tone.

DiMachio's eyes narrowed and his hands clenched into fists. He looked angrily from one executive to the next, his eyes finally resting on Langley. DiMachio glared in silence as he watched Langley avoid his stare and light up another cigarette. After several drags and many long seconds of avoidance, DiMachio made brief eye contact with Senior Senior Executive President of Business Affairs and Law, and General Counsel, Langley. Langley turned away nervously and lit another cigarette, each of his hands now holding a burning tobacco stick. DiMachio remained deathly silent and continued boring into Langley.

Langley had four cigarettes burning before he succumbed to DiMachio's malicious scrutiny. He looked through his wall of smoke and returned DiMachio's gaze.

"Is there something we've overlooked, DiMachio?" he asked, his smoke cloud trembling.

"Is there something we overlooked?" DiMachio sarcastically mocked, his emotional stove turned to high, his fluids once again beginning to boil. He stared with hatred at each of his executive staff and slowly repeated his words. "Is there something we overlooked?!" DiMachio pounded his clenched fist on the table and rose to his full five-feet, seven-inch height, not waiting for a flimsy reply. "Yes, god damn it, there is something someone overlooked!" He glared at the executives seated in fear around the table, his nostrils flaring and steam once again beginning to escape his ears and nose. "Do any of you know what's happened with Big?"

"Well, DiMachio," said Derby, his ornate silver fork trembling behind his ear. "We just told you..."

"That's not what I mean!" DiMachio screamed. "I don't give a fuck right now about status reports and his sales levels!"

The four executives shrunk a good two feet in fear, their chins almost resting on the table.

"One of you imbeciles, one of you moronic imbeciles, forgot to consider the fact there are armies, and I mean armed and dangerous armies, of entertainment lawyers out there. And it seems our contract with Big didn't cover the possibility that he might be approached in private by an outside attorney and sign a contract with him!"

Weena pointed to Langley. "That's Langley's job. He should have thought of that."

"Yeah," said Derby as he pointed at the Business Affairs and Law executive. "Langley."

Jiglio stared at Langley, a small smirk playing at the corners of his mouth.

DiMachio pounded the table once again, the angry, malicious sound making each of the executives shrink four more inches. "I know whose job it is, damn it. I also know I hired an executive team to work together. I hold all of you responsible for this, not just Langley."

Langley sighed discreetly and grew an inch.

"What happened?" asked Jiglio.

"What happened," said DiMachio in a mocking tone. "Is that Bret Horowitz, entertainment lawyer and general legal scum, somehow got to Big and signed him on as a client. And Harvey Gildsteen managed to leech on as his manager."

"How does that affect things?" asked Weena.

DiMachio sat down, his anger still seething. "It means we have to endure one of the most horrendous ordeals a record company can go through."

"Which is?" asked Derby.

"A RENEGOTIATION, you moron," screamed DiMachio. "We have to renegotiate the contract. And with that leech of a lawyer prowling around out there, we'll be sucked dry of all our extra bonuses and monetary compensation for dealing with a clonebot!"

Langley took a drag from each of his lit cigarettes and exhaled a protective cloud of smoke. "DiMachio, there would have been a renegotiation anyway. Big's gone platinum; he's sold so many records it's inevitable his lawyers and manager would want to renegotiate. Every musician who has a hit record demands a contract negotiation."

DiMachio pounded his fist on the table. "But, you moron, Big never had a lawyer or manager! We drafted the contract ourselves. Someone should have realized that legal slime could infiltrate."

Langley puffed away on his cigarettes, enveloping himself behind a thicker and thicker cloud of smoke. "You know as well as I that if an entertainment lawyer wanted him that badly, they'd do anything to get him, regardless. It's not our fault."

DiMachio leaned forward and thrust his finger toward Langley's face. "I can damn well blame whoever I want! I'm the ruling dictator around here. And don't forget it!"

Jiglio rubbed the bulging red boil on his forehead, his eyes steely black and, as always, full of ice. "What are you so concerned about? That Horowitz will find out Big's a clonebot?"

"No!" DiMachio bellowed back.

"Then what's the problem?" said Weena as she ran her fingers through her very thin and almost bald black Brillo pad hair.

DiMachio threw his hands up in exasperation. "You people don't get this, do you?"

"Get what?" said Derby.

"Grasp the fact, you moron, that we have just lost control of our artist. The Yakadans convinced us we could program Big to our needs, that we could tell him what to do and how to act, and he would follow every order to the letter, meaning we could make literally millions and millions of dollars off him."

"But we've already told him what to do and how to act," said Jiglio.

"That's not the point!" DiMachio barked. "The point is that Horowitz and Gildsteen can program him against us. And the Yakadans don't care. They're more interested in their robots and clones and whatever mutant life forms they're creating than in selling music.

And I," continued the Deity, pointing to his chest. "Am much more interested in making money than in any machine. The Yakadans said they could study him under any condition, so I'm sure they'd prefer Big to have outside counsel because they're trying to make this experiment as life and humanlike as possible."

"But if the Yakadans don't mind," Weena began.

"The Yakadans don't matter!" DiMachio screamed. "We've lost control. We could program Big to our needs. We were getting unheard of royalties, increasing our year-end bonuses. We were becoming rich off this machine. But that's gone. We have to treat him like we do all our prima donna superstars. We'll have to cater to him, be nice to him, treat him with respect." DiMachio looked up to the ceiling and shook his clasped hands. "I thought it was going to be simple."

He looked around the table at four fearful, yet blank, faces. His staff wasn't getting it and weren't grasping the amount of money DiMachio could have made. How could he have surrounded himself with such idiots.

"Get out!" he bellowed. "Just get the hell out of my office and go work for a change!"

He rose from his throne and stormed over to his Acht transmobile. By the time Heysannah reached the driver's seat and began chauffeuring him back to his desk, DiMachio felt the emptiness created by his staff's departure.

Dropping, dismissing, firing, and terminating became DiMachio's four favorite words, so much so that he took to a little corporate shuffling and reorganization every morning. The people were merely positions, the bands most certainly replaceable, and it was the power of control DiMachio loved more and more as he changed the fate of people's lives with one slash of his pen, or one phone call to the right person.

His loss of control over Big's future had made him obsessed with power, so much so he began to feel invincible; he began to feel he was a Deity, a god ordained to mold and shape the world's musical map.

What was once an ego inflated with the rock and roll lifestyle became an impenetrable barricade built from hatred, rage, and jealousy. It was an obsession that overpowered his inbred paranoia and caution, made him reckless and inattentive to his executive surveillance monitors, and made him vulnerable to corporate predators.

Eleven

The electrified neck shocks jerked Alex's head to the right and left, her blonde hair flying about her as it began to streak stress magenta and depressed blue. Langley hadn't returned yet from his impromptu, confidential meeting with the other Senior Senior Executive Presidents in DiMachio's office, yet Alex's neck was having electrified spasms like never before, the message being clear; Langley wanted her in his office immediately.

Alex felt her way around her desk, her head performing its own uncontrollable dance, and entered Langley's domain. She sunk onto her secretarial steno stool and held her head between her hands, trying to quell the spasms.

Alex heard another elevator full of corporate paper pushers and overworked, frazzled administrative assistants scurrying up and down the hall, delivering their bosses' everything-I-write-is-urgent-because-I'm-so-important memos. Alex heard the thunderous, crashing sound coming toward her and knew Langley was making his way to the office. Through her spasmodic neck shocks, she saw him storm through the door, his eyes bulging out a good six inches from his face, his neck purple and ready to explode. He rushed behind his desk and fell into his chair, his hands releasing the electrified secretary shocker control panel.

Alex's neck stopped jerking from side to side, but her eyes still swayed with the momentum from the jolts. She held tightly to the bottom of her stool and thought herself out of her dizziness and nausea, no small feat without a brain.

Langley opened his desk drawer and slammed it shut with such force his pencil holder tipped over, breaking several points off his perfectly sharpened Ticonderoga number two pencils. He stood up and clenched his fists. "I've had it with you and these damn pencils!" he screamed in Alex's face. He closed his eyes and stomped his feet in a kindergarten temper tantrum. "Had it! Had it!" He slammed his clenched fists on his desk. "Can't you keep these things sharpened and on my desk?!"

Alex closed her eyes and took a deep breath. She reflexively reached into her pocket, but it was empty. She searched through her other pocket but all she found was a stiff, crumpled up tissue. Terror shot through her body. She was out of candy. She must have forgotten to fill her pockets that morning.

She looked at her boss, adrenaline coursing through her veins and her body aching for some refined white sugar.

When she didn't reply, Langley clenched his fists tighter and banged on his desk harder. "Have you nothing to say?!" he screamed.

Alex desperately searched through her pockets again, but they were empty. Her breath came in short gasps as emotion started to pulsate throughout her body. And she didn't like what she was feeling. Every cell in her body screamed for chocolate to drown her anger in. She shivered as a cold rage seeped into her heart and began to fill her body. Her muscles tightened, her jaw clamped, and she glared at Langley.

The vein in his forehead visibly pounded. Langley's eyes bulged even further as he shook with an all-consuming, uncontrollable rage. Alex instinctively stood and moved backward. The veins on both sides of his neck exploded with such force that blood shot across the room and splattered both walls, running down to the floor in streams. Langley clutched both sides of his neck, red ooze spilling out from between his fingers, and fell back into his chair.

"Sutures," he croaked as his shirt became drenched with blood.

Alex ran to her desk, breathing heavily. The screaming, the blood, the prison she had forced herself into. She put her hand on her desk to steady herself as she panted harder and harder. She ripped open her drawers but couldn't find a piece of candy, not even a stick of gum. All her time at Acht flashed before her eyes – the humiliation, the mistreatment, the utter disregard for her feelings. She had to find some chocolate and find it soon. She felt her stomach boiling with anger, and her body shook with rage.

"ALEX!" blew out the door.

The anger hit her in the face and knocked the breath out of her. She felt her neck pounding and felt the pressure in her stomach shoot up through her body. She let out a loud scream as her own neck exploded with blood. It shot across her desk and covered her computer. She fell back into her chair, seized with terror. She clutched her neck with one hand and reached for the emergency suturing kit.

Another hand took it from her.

"I knew this was going to happen someday," said Hellie as she covered herself with a protective surgical gown and opened the kit. She expertly threaded the needle.

Alex looked at Hellie speechless.

Hellie smiled. "So, I took an emergency suturing course the other week." She expertly applied the local anesthetic and quickly sewed Alex up. She gently wrapped sterile gauze around Alex's neck, knotting the front into an almost-stylish looking scarf.

"Thanks," said Alex, her voice uncharacteristically hard. She stood and felt what little blood was left drain from her face.

"Stay here," said Hellie. "I'll do Langley."

"No," said Alex harshly. "For your own good, don't get involved."

Hellie reached under her gown and pulled something out of her pocket. "Then, here," she said as she pulled out an orange and quickly peeled and quartered it. "Eat this."

Alex took a piece of the orange and put it into her mouth. When the dizziness subsided, she stood, her body cold and hard. "I'll take care of Langley. Go back to your desk, and don't let anyone know what you can do."

"But I want to…"

"No," exclaimed Alex once again. "This is my mess. And it's about time I cleaned it up."

Alex glared at Hellie until the receptionist left the suite and headed down the hall. Alex picked up the emergency suturing kit and walked into Langley's office.

"Sutures," was all that escaped Langley's mouth as blood soaked through his clothes and oozed onto his desk and chair.

Alex opened her first aid kit and pulled out the heavy-duty suturing thread and needle she used for especially bad eruptions. She threaded the needle and jabbed hard through Langley's skin, not bothering to apply the local anesthetic lotion.

"Ahhh!!"

"Oh, don't be a baby," said Alex coldly. "You should be used to this by now."

Langley turned to her with a murderous glare, his body and clothes covered in blood. "You…"

"Don't 'you' me, Langley. Or I'll make sure you lose more blood." Alex leaned in front of Langley and looked into his eyes, a cold smile crossing her face. "And you might die if we're not careful." Alex straightened and pulled the suturing thread slowly through her boss' skin, savoring the pain she felt erupting from his flesh.

"If you so much…"

Alex stopped sewing and put her hands on her hips. She spoke in a semi-scolding, harshly patronizing tone. "Now, Langley, if you keep talking, you'll distract me, and who knows what could happen. I might pierce another vein, or accidentally cut you."

She saw Langley stiffen and noticed what looked like fear in his eyes.

Alex pulled the thread hard, making sure to give an extra yank, and expertly sewed her perfect, special, modified X over the top backstitch. She rammed the needle into his flesh, making sure Langley felt every excruciating, torturous second. He moaned in agony, his eyes rolling to the back of his head, as she yanked and jabbed, punctured and pulled.

Alex finished her work and covered her mending job with first aid bandages.

"There we go," she said as she stepped back to survey her work. "I think you'll make it." She smiled icily. "This time."

"You did that on purpose," Langley moaned weakly.

"Don't be silly," said Alex as she leaned in front of his face, staring him straight in the eye. "That was a major eruption, and you know those are hard to close up. I'm just doing the job you make me do."

Langley glared at her but said nothing. Alex watched his face with a cold satisfaction, knowing the exact lack of coloring for a blood infusion, but not caring if he needed one.

"Make sure those pencils are sharpened," said Langley feebly as he swung around in his chair, the back of the leather throne-in-waiting facing Alex.

Alex's body tingled with an almost perverse delight as she experienced her first rush of misdirected anger. The power was almost an aphrodisiac. She felt something dark try to take root inside her as she returned to her desk, the pencils left broken and spilled on her boss' blotter. She was past caring.

Twelve

"Zena, honey, come here for a minute," Jiglio called through his office door one afternoon. He sat back and watched with male enjoyment as his leggy, lingerie-clad secretary slunk into the room, her black purple washed hair falling forward on her face and tickling her exposed cleavage. His icy black eyes and steely demeanor melted as he burned with an animal passion only a man could feel for the exposed flesh and voluptuous bosom of a sexually ready young woman.

"Hi, Jiggy," Zena purred after she shut the door, as she was always instructed to do.

She swished over to his desk. "Is there something you need?"

She walked behind his chair, as she did every time she came to see him and reached around the leather to massage his shoulders.

Senior Senior Executive President of Promotion Jiglio leaned back, far enough so his chair angled just below her breasts. He felt them above his head, warm, full, and inviting. Zena's hands worked their way from his shoulders to his neck, then wandered down the front of his shirt, seeking the prize that lay stiffened with excitement between his legs. Jiglio moaned with desire, wanting it, needing it, as he believed every man needed no-commitment sex, but he also knew he could get it whenever he wanted.

He gently covered Zena's hands and squeezed, stopping her as she reached his zipper.

"Zena, honey, I have something really important I need you to do."

Zena lowered her mouth to his ear. "Anything, Jiggy. Anything for you."

Jiglio lifted Zena's arms above his head and guided her from behind his chair to his favorite spot on his desk. He sat her down on his desk blotter and slowly spread open her legs, checking to make sure she had removed her panties that morning, as he had instructed her to do every day when she arrived at work. Some mornings he removed them himself and kept them in his top drawer to fondle and sniff all day long.

Jiglio stared into the depths of Zena's womanliness, his hands gently squeezing the soft, white flesh of her inner thighs. His best friend cried out to be relieved, aching with a longing for penetration, but more important matters were at stake that morning. He reluctantly removed his hands and opened his desk drawer. He pulled out a sealed, fattened envelope, handing it to his secretary.

"Honey, I need you to do me a favor." He smiled coyly. "It's spy time again. Remember? Like the other times?"

"Sure, Jiggy, I remember," Zena cooed as she took the envelope and spread her legs open a bit further. "I play spy for you, do whatever you tell me, ask no questions, never tell anyone, and then I get my reward."

Jiglio ran his hand up Zena's thigh, feeling her pulsating warmth and wet invitation. "Exactly, my sweet. I need you to take the envelope and go outside the building. There'll be a big, black car waiting for you. The driver knows what you look like, so when you see him get out and open the door, get in. Don't talk to him. Don't ask questions." The promotion executive's fingers teased Zena. "Do you understand me so far, honey?"

Zena tilted her head back and moaned, spreading her legs further apart as she invited her boss to enter her.

Jiglio stood and pressed his stiffened member against her. He leaned into her ear and whispered, "Zena, honey, this is important. Do you understand?"

Zena thrust her pelvis toward him and moaned again. "Yes, Jiggy, I'll make you proud." Her breath came in gasps as she looked into her boss' eyes. "I saw a beautiful mink coat in Bantham's yesterday."

Jiglio reluctantly sat down and smiled at his secretary. "Mink would look beautiful on you."

Zena squealed with joy and wrapped her legs around her boss' neck. "Oh, Jiggy, you make me so horny. Take me now," she purred.

Jiglio grabbed Zena's legs as they tightened around his neck and pulled him in toward her wet, warm, pulsating mound of femininity. He wavered for a moment, swept up in his desire, and nearly dove in

102

headfirst. With superhuman effort, Jiglio unwrapped Zena's legs from around his head and rolled back in his chair.

"Zena, honey," he said, panting with unfulfilled passion. He pushed her legs together and moaned with sexual frustration. "We've got to do this first, okay?"

Zena nodded and sat up straight.

Jiglio rolled his chair closer to his secretary. "Listen carefully. The car will take off and drive a little way, probably a few blocks. Hand the envelope to the man driving the car, but don't say anything. He'll take it and bring you back to the building."

The promotion man winked at Zena as his hand slid across her breast. "I shouldn't tell you, but your secret mission is going to help a very, very, very big artist."

Zena smiled. "Oh, who, Jiggy, who?"

Senior Senior Executive President of Promotion Jiglio petted his secretary's cheek. "If I could tell you, honey, I would. You know that." He put his finger to his lips. "But it's a big secret. I shouldn't have told you this much, so you'll have to trust me. Okay, sweetheart?"

The lingerie-clad secretary nodded.

"And you understand everything I told you?"

Zena leaned forward and ran her hands up and down her boss' neck. "Of course I do. Don't worry; you'll be proud of me."

Jiglio bent forward and kissed his secretary's inner thigh. "I'm always proud of you, honey."

"And I'll look beautiful in that mink coat."

Jiglio placed his hands on Zena's knees and slowly closed her legs. "Especially with nothing on underneath," he muttered. Jiglio rolled back his chair and pulled Zena to her feet. With a playful smack on her backside, he shooed her out of his office. "Now, go."

After she'd left, Jiglio leaned back in his chair and glared through the ice that had reformed in his eyes. DiMachio asked for it; DiMachio had it coming. An evil smile found its way onto his face.

*

As Zena drove around the city on her secret mission, DiMachio stared out his executive window onto the city before him, waiting for his

103

daily company report so he could plan his next sabotage attack. He glanced at his watch and then quickly looked at the digital clock on the MONY building. Accurate again. He turned his back to the window. When he glanced at his desk, he realized his report had appeared, again on time. Maybe his assistants were getting too good; he might have to do something about them. He sat down in his fur lined gilt trimmed leather throne and shuffled through the pages, looking for any excuse to terminate, cancel or change anything before him.

The Deity reached the page of new releases and glanced through the list of records being released that week.

"What the hell," he said.

He picked up his phone and dialed the Senior Senior Executive President of A&R's extension. "Skeater, it's DiMachio," he barked into the phone. "What's this Latitude Repellent crap that came out this week."

"It's Platitude Rebellion," said Skeater from the other end.

"What is it?" asked the Deity.

"They're my latest signing. I played their CD for you a month or two back. You okayed it."

"I don't remember."

"I came to your office. You weren't sure about them, but when I came back and told you I'd go on a hunger strike or leave the company if you didn't sign them, you agreed I could take them on."

DiMachio begrudgingly remembered. "Well, they better start selling or they're history." He slammed down the phone. He punched another extension on his speaker phone.

"Weena, it's DiMachio." The Deity heard a thud over the phone line and knew a random body part had just hit the Senior Senior Executive President of Media Relations' desk. "Big. What's new with Big."

"He's got ten interviews this week, two talk shows, and a brief appearance on VH1."

"Not enough! Big is top priority. I want that asshole to make millions of dollars for us. I want to squeeze every penny out of him that we can. You hear me?"

"Yes," squeaked over the line.

"Milk Big until he's dry. Keep him interviewing twenty hours a day if you have to. Make him bigger than Elvis. I want him so famous he won't be able to leave his house."

DiMachio slammed off his speakerphone and leaned back in his throne. He might not have full control of Big anymore; he might not have all the royalty points he once had, but DiMachio planned to make him so famous the clonebot would blow a few circuits. The Deity laughed his first evil laugh in months.

*

Skeater hung up the phone and shut his eyes, massaging his aching temples. DiMachio had been on a rampage, dropping bands right and left, which he frequently did, but this time it was with a vengeance. Unrecouped bands, bands not making the money back that was spent upfront for them, were often let out of their contract, but when the Deity started asking about new bands, bands that had released albums only weeks earlier, something was wrong.

Skeater rolled back his chair, unable to stay seated any longer. It used to be fun, signing bands, going on the road, traveling the world. He had felt part of something, part of a large family of musicians around the world. But since he'd become successful and signed several multi-platinum acts, and was promoted into essentially a paperwork desk job, Skeater's life had changed. Work had become more routine, the challenge was gone, and there was an emptiness that followed him around. He picked up Skat and left his office, knowing a walk outside would help clear his head. As Skeater made his way to the elevator, he knew he couldn't complain. His salary, with bonuses and extra perks added, was over a million dollars a year. Certainly not bad for a thirty-five-year-old. But something was missing.

When the elevator doors slid open, he was pleasantly surprised to see Langley's assistant standing in the car. He felt his heart skip a beat, felt an excitement he hadn't felt since he'd signed his first band.

"Hi, Alex," he said as he stepped in and pushed the lobby button.

Alex's stress magenta and cold gray hair became highlighted with the purple Skeater was becoming accustomed to seeing.

"Hi, Skeater," she said as she turned and stared at the descending numbers.

Skeater took a slow, deep breath, wondering how to talk to her without making a total fool of himself. He looked at her beautifully sad face and her ocean blue eyes and noticed a difference in her, an edge that hadn't been there before. It saddened him. He fought back the urge to touch her.

"How's it going?"

Alex shrugged. "Okay, I guess. I'm on another memo delivery run." She glanced up in Skeater's direction with a forced smile.

"Doesn't Langley use email?"

Alex shook her head and looked hard at the elevator doors. "Don't get me started. He can't use a computer, refuses to learn, and refuses to let me send emails for him."

Skeater shook his head. "Unbelievable."

"You can say that again," said Alex.

*

The elevator stopped on the seventeenth floor. When the doors opened, a whirlwind of repressed energy zipped into the car, emitting a short, dry cough. He handed a cassette to both Skeater and Alex.

"Clef," said Skeater with delight to the gangly Roadrunner of Rock. "Great to see you."

"Skeater, Skeater, a pleasure."

Clef shook Skeater's hand and pushed a button, nervously bouncing around the car.

"Have you ever met Alex?" Skeater asked the Indie Kingpin and Roadrunner of Rock.

"No, no, never met," said Clef as he held out his hand.

"Hi," said Alex as she responded to his gesture. "I've seen you around the building." She glanced at his beekeeper outfit, complete with hood and miniature fake bees glued all over the bee suit and didn't have to look at the casing of the cassette to know the name of the band.

The bell rang, signaling its arrival one flight down. Clef coughed his short, dry cough, waved his farewell, and zipped out of the elevator, armed and prepared to hand out cassettes to any passerby.

When the doors closed, Alex and Skeater were again left alone in an unspoken silence.

"Great guy, that Clef," said Skeater.

"Hmm." Alex leaned against the elevator wall. "But why does he wear those strange outfits?"

Skeater laughed. "It's a gimmick."

"A gimmick?"

Skeater shifted Skat to his other arm and leaned against the wall next to Alex. "There's so much music released here that Clef's bands sometimes get lost in the shuffle. So, he has to do whatever he can to get attention to his music."

"You mean those outfits help him?"

Skeater smiled. "In a way, yes. It's easier to remember which bands are his. And when records are being prioritized for marketing and promotion, it can make a difference."

"Who would have thought?"

The bell rang, and the elevator doors opened. Alex looked briefly at Skeater. "Nice talkin' to you." She strode out of the car and headed down the hall.

"Alex..."

Alex turned and saw Skeater standing hesitantly in the elevator, looking unsure of himself, so much like a child. Alex felt her new-found hardness melt a little as he stood looking at her with his mouth open and no words coming out. A wave of self-consciousness washed over her.

*

Skeater stared at Alex, his body and mouth frozen. She was looking at him, waiting patiently for him to speak, but he couldn't get a word out of his mouth. The doors closed, the elevator dropping to the ground floor, taking Skeater's sinking heart along with it.

Thirteen

"Alex!"

Alex glanced up from her computer screen and looked around. Her secretarial outer office area was empty. She knew it wasn't Langley. Big's renegotiation had begun several weeks ago, and her boss had decided to live in the thirty-fifth-floor conference room. Gave him an edge, he had said. Better focus. Langley could work twenty-four hours a day, with no time-wasting commutes or general office distractions. The only time Alex saw him was when he shocked her to bring him fresh blood and sutures. And that suited her just fine.

She returned to work and concentrated on typing Langley's A, B, C list of favorite New York hospitals and emergency rooms, including doctors on duty, specialists on board, and general surgical procedures. Langley had to be prepared, especially since he'd started erupting several times a day.

"Alex, listen to me."

Again, Alex looked around her office suite. She was not finding it funny. "Zena, if this is some kind of game, stop right now. I'm not amused."

"Alex!"

Alex typed harder. If this turned out to be some kind of prank, the joke was not going to be on Alex.

"Hey, Alex, I'm here."

Alex felt her now-familiar anger begin to simmer. She let out an exasperated sigh.

"Psst, Alex, here."

"Who are you?" she barked.

"Who do you think I am?"

Alex spun around in her chair and faced her empty office area. "Where the hell are you?"

"Here, right next to you."

Alex looked to both sides and still saw nothing. She looked under her desk, around her desk, in her desk, but still found nothing. She sat back in her seat. "I'm going crazy, that's all there is to it."

"No, you're not."

"Damn it!" said Alex to her empty secretarial suite. "Who's there?"

"Me," came in reply. "Or you. Whatever you want to call us."

Alex froze. It couldn't be. It was impossible, absolutely impossible.

"No, actually, it is possible."

Alex shakily looked to her left, her eyes resting on her mandatory synthetic crystal cerebrum urn. Inside, swimming in clear nutrient juice, her brain throbbed and pulsated in what she could only call delightful glee.

Alex's cerebral cortex straightened in the urn. Her brain stem gave her a cheerful wave. "Hello. It's about time you noticed me. I've been trying to get your attention for a long time."

"But, but," stammered Alex. "You're my brain, you can't talk."

"Maybe not to other people, but I can certainly talk to you." Alex's brain back flipped with joy. "And, boy, do I have a lot to say."

Alex was speechless. She had to be going crazy.

Her brain stopped doing its joyful jig and looked at her intently. "You're not crazy, Alex. You're far from it. You're actually one of the sanest people here."

Alex let out an exasperated sigh. "If this is sane, I'd hate to see crazy."

Her brain settled to the bottom of the urn, her wrinkled looking, hot dog colored cerebral cortex drooping a little. "I can see this is going to be a challenge."

"What's going to be a challenge?" asked Alex.

"Getting you to understand."

"To understand what?"

Alex's brain flipped upside down and slowly floated to the top of the urn. "I can't tell you."

Alex leaned in closer, the muscles in her face rigid and tense. "What's the point of having this discussion if you can't tell me?"

Her brain turned on its side and swam in circles around the synthetic crystal Acht container.

"What's the point in telling you anything if you're not ready to understand?"

Alex's voice began to rise in pitch. "How do you know I can't understand something unless you tell me what it is?"

Her brain swam faster. "If you understood, you wouldn't have asked that question."

"But I don't know what the question is!" exclaimed Alex as she crossed her arms.

Her brain stopped swimming and pressed up against the glass, as if it was looking at Alex. "Then how can you understand the answer?"

Alex sat back in her chair and let out an exasperated sigh. "How did I end up with you for a brain?"

Alex's brain began bouncing up and down. "If I didn't know you so well, I might be offended."

Alex shook her head. "Only me."

Her brain looked at her sternly. "Stop that."

Alex looked at her urn in surprise. "Stop what?"

"When you put me back in, think about it, and answer your own question."

Alex felt her face begin to flush with anger. "I told you, I don't know the question."

Her brain continued to bob in its nutrient juice. "Then figure it out."

Alex uncrossed her arms and smiled, momentarily forgetting to be angry. "I might be getting it. I never asked the right questions; I was too busy looking for answers."

Her brain bounced happily in the urn. "We're making progress."

Alex leaned forward. "Once I figure out the right questions to ask, the answers will come."

Alex paused for a moment, then smiled. "Even better, the questions might already be there too. It's simply a matter of uncovering them."

"Better," said her brain. "There's one thing I can tell you right now. They can take away your ability to think; they can strip you of your thoughts, but no company, no conglomeration, can take away your ability to be. Unless you let them."

"What if I don't know how to stop them?"

Her brain curved into what looked like a smile. "You must know something. We wouldn't be having this conversation if you didn't."

Alex stared at her urn. "I still don't understand why you're here, especially now."

"Because you decided to start listening." Her brain stood erect in the urn. Alex's right hemisphere inflated to almost twice its size, then slowly shrunk back to its original shape. Her left hemisphere followed, inflating and deflating. Her brain repeated the movements, first the right hemisphere, then the left. "Anger isn't always a bad thing. If used properly, it can help you open doors to new parts of yourself. And I'm here to help."

"Took you long enough," said Alex as she watched her cerebrum swelling and shrinking, expanding and contracting.

"Didn't take any time at all. You're the one who walked away."

Alex could have sworn her brain was getting out of breath.

"So, this is my fault?"

"No, it was your choice. No one forced you here, but here you are. You're unhappy, and you've done everything you can do. What does that mean?"

"That I need to get out of here."

"Maybe. What's important is that you're finally ready to listen to yourself. I didn't suddenly come to you; I've been here all along. You finally decided to try listening." Her brain bounced and inflated, spun around and deflated.

"What in the world are you doing?" Alex blurted out.

Her brain stopped flexing and floated in the nutrient juice. "Doing what?"

"All that jumping around. You look like there's something wrong."

"I'm exercising," her brain replied.

"Aren't I the one who should be exercising?"

"Body, mind, it's all the same. I need a workout as much as you." Her brain resumed its acrobatics. "And lord knows I haven't had much exercise since you came to this place."

Alex smiled wryly. "You can say that again."

If a brain could smile, hers was positively beaming. "But that's all about to change." Her cerebrum stopped momentarily and faced her. "One word of advice. Be careful what you wish for. It might not be what you really want."

"Don't worry, I know what I want," said Alex.

"We'll see," was her brain's last comment before it resumed its rigorous workout routine.

Alex turned back to her computer and continued typing. She smiled deeply for the first time in months. Maybe things would be okay after all.

*

DiMachio sat in his corporate kingdom. He stood in his corporate kingdom. He paced up and down in his corporate kingdom. He walked to his outer office and saw his Swedish blonde Doublemint twins of rock sitting behind their desks, answering phones, fending off unwanted employees, processing mountains of paperwork. Overcome with playfulness, and urged on by Jeremy Wickett, DiMachio walked around their long, two-person desk and unzipped his fly.

"Hey, little girls, want some candy?" asked Deity and Ruling Dictator DiMachio as he exposed himself and swung Jeremy Wickett to and fro.

"Put it away, DiMachio," said Heysannah with the boredom of having witnessed the display before.

"Girlies, come on. Jeremy wants you."

Deity DiMachio wiggled himself around, prancing and preening, until he realized neither twin was interested in what he and Jeremy had to offer. Bored, he entered his kingdom and sat down in his fur lined gilt trimmed leather throne and yawned an executive boardroom yawn, the kind of yawn a much-too-powerful man would emit when his day was empty of conquests and slayings.

It was eleven in the morning, and DiMachio had already ordered two up-and-coming executives fired, citing departmental reorganization as the reason, but knowing they were too aggressive and moving too fast through the corporate ranks. He had also yelled at his private chef and waiter; his scrambled eggs had been too dry and his orange juice too cold. He stared at the wall fifty feet across his office and noticed Hosannah and Heysannah had tacked up the daily updated artist roster, as he had recently instructed them to do each morning. The pages were tacked up in military order, the rows and columns perfectly aligned, an exact one-inch wall space around each edge.

"Time for some corporate trimming," said DiMachio with malevolent glee. Jeremy responded with stiffened excitement and growing anticipation.

Deity DiMachio reached under his desk and pulled out his air-pumped, metal BB gun. He hit his speakerphone intercom. "Heysannah, get in here now!"

The door cautiously opened, not because it was heavy or hard to move, but because DiMachio had started hurling heavy objects around the room at his assistants. After a lead crystal ashtray hit Hosannah in the stomach and knocked the wind out of her, both assistants checked to make sure DiMachio was unarmed. Heysannah looked both ways, then scurried over to his side, her eyes unfocussed and staring straight ahead.

DiMachio handed her his rifle. "Pump."

Heysannah unlatched the metal rod on the barrel of the gun and began pumping air into the rifle. When she reached the proper tension, she obediently handed the gun back to DiMachio. The Deity lifted the rifle up to his shoulders and peered through the eyesight. The print was impossible to read, but DiMachio could see the black ink that listed the names of his artists, row after row, page after page. DiMachio took aim and fired the gun. A BB shot across the room and tore through one of the rows, a direct hit.

"Yes!" said DiMachio as he handed the gun back to Heysannah. "Pump."

Heysannah complied, once more pumping pressure into the rifle. She handed the gun back to DiMachio, who again fired another shot at the wall.

"Damn it," the Deity and Ruling Dictator cursed as the metal ball veered slightly to the right and embedded itself into the wall.

Heysannah took the gun from her boss and pumped. When ready, she handed it back.

Jeremy looked on in excitement as DiMachio took aim and fired a direct hit. "Two down," he said jovially as he gave Jeremy a satisfied pat and handed the gun back to his executive assistant.

Eight more times Heysannah pumped, and eight more times DiMachio fired.

"That's it for today," said Deity and Ruling Dictator DiMachio after he hit his fifth target. He put the bee bee gun under his desk and pointed toward the wall. "Get rid of them."

Heysannah hurried over and removed the pages. She returned to her desk to phone five managers and tell them their band was no longer on the label.

Deity DiMachio drummed his fingers on the jewel-encrusted armrest of his throne, bored again and impatiently waiting for his next malevolent inspiration. He stared out his window across the concrete landscape, then quickly checked his watch. The building clock was still accurate. He leaned over and thumbed through his executive surveillance files; nothing new since the day before. He and Jeremy Wickett had already gone a few rounds, but self-gratification could be unsatisfying if overused.

DiMachio punched the intercom button on his speakerphone. "Heysannah, Hosannah, whoever's out there, get in my office!"

Before DiMachio could punch off, both six-foot tall, Swedish blonde assistants sprang through the doorway, alert and cautious to possible UFOs, and whizzed over to his desk.

"You wanted us, Mr. Deity?" the twins asked in vacant unison.

DiMachio looked at them with near contempt, as he did to all women. "Of course I wanted you, you incompetent morons; otherwise, I wouldn't have called you in here."

Both young women remained silent, speaking the only common language of their gender.

DiMachio quickly checked his watch and was disappointed to once again find the exact time on the clock atop the skyscraper outside his window. "What's on my agenda for today? Anything interesting?"

Heysannah opened her steno pad and scanned down the day's events. "You had your breakfast. Lunch is at one-thirty; you're dining alone with Jeremy Wickett, and you have dinner reservations at seven at Nobu. You canceled your two meetings for today, so unless you want to sign paperwork, your schedule is open."

Realizing there was nothing left to dominate, executive boredom set in again. He glanced again at his docile-looking, war weary assistants. "What's going on in the company today? There must be something happening I can take part in."

Hosannah opened her Acht corporate steno pad and scanned through the day's major events at the company. "At eleven thirty, Jiglio will be ordering one of his eight vice presidents to fire five regional promotional people."

DiMachio dismissed the suggestion with a wave of his hand. "Already fired people today."

"At one, the Corporate Communications department is holding a press conference, announcing the formation of the Vincent DiMachio Children's Aid Society, a charitable organization set up to aid homeless and poor children around the world."

The Deity rolled his eyes. "Absolutely not. Giving my name was enough." DiMachio's fidgeting became more agitated. "There has to be *something* going on in this company."

Hosannah continued reading through her list. "New technologies demonstration, virtual reality, and home concerts."

"No."

"Platitude Rebellion will be in the media relations department today, doing phone interviews."

"Whoever the hell they are. I'll see them if I hand them gold and platinum records. That's enough."

"A new band signing. Moss Pus. At three."

"No!"

Hosannah continued down her list. "Big's renegotiation is wrapping up this week. Today might be the last day."

DiMachio consulted with Jeremy, a smirk spreading its way across his face. "Yes, Big's renegotiation. I must take part in that."

DiMachio stood and walked toward his Acht transmobile. "Hosannah, get my temporary throne installed in the renegotiation room, but don't say why." He brushed off the first Swedish-blonde twin and waved over the second. "Heysannah, get your ass in the cart and take me to this meeting."

Fourteen

Renegotiations were ruthless, but even DiMachio, the Deity of corporate warfare, was shocked as he crossed the threshold of the thirty-fifth-floor conference room. Several weeks of constant Langley explosions had turned the regulation gray walls a permanent shade of red; nothing could remove the blood stains, except perhaps a few coats of thick, industrial strength paint. Coagulated blobs of Langley's life juice had formed randomly throughout the room, leaving gelatinous mounds of wobbly blood dangling precariously from the ceiling and walls.

DiMachio carefully stepped into the room and walked over to his throne-on-the-go, his mobile, on wheels, fur lined gilt trimmed leather throne that appeared before him in every meeting off the executive floor.

As he approached his chair, he glanced up and saw a large hemorrhoid-like sac of blood dislodge from the ceiling and career toward his head. DiMachio jumped to the right just in time. The blood splattered onto the floor, narrowly missing his hand stitched, custom-made designer Italian suit. He stepped over the pool of blood spreading across the floor and sat down in his throne, pulling out his microcassette recorder.

"Install umbrella or canopy over throne."

Deity DiMachio pocketed his tape recorder and looked at the eight lawyers staring at him in silence. He saw the strain of renegotiation in their haggard looks and bleary eyes, yet he still sensed an underlying current of evil, lawyer determination.

"Well, carry on," said DiMachio with his characteristic irritation.

Bret Horowitz, entertainment lawyer, turned back to Langley who sat partially mummified, swaths of blood-soaked white gauze wrapped crazily all over his body. "Where were we?" he asked, his box of manufactured smiles locked away for the duration of the renegotiation, his lips a tight, straight line of seriousness. He was flanked on his right by two lawyers from his firm, their main duty to sit next to him and give his side power in numbers. To the entertainment lawyer's left sat one of his partners, Willard Gardner, there to assist Horowitz in negotiation and intimidation. All four lawyers leaned forward, their elbows on the table, as they waited for the opposing team's volley.

Langley was surrounded by three lawyers from the legal side of his department, their job to draft the contract being renegotiated and to even out the number of bodies across the table. Senior Senior Executive President of Business Affairs and Law, and General Counsel, Langley took a drag off one of the three cigarettes he had burning in his ashtray. "Master reversion, our last major point," blew out of his mouth with a cloud of smoke.

"Right," said Horowitz, his eyes narrowing for battle. "We're holding at seven."

"We're firm at twenty-five," said Langley.

"Langley," DiMachio hissed, motioning his senior executive over to his throne.

Langley rose and made his way over to his Deity, momentarily thrown off balance as he skidded through the puddle of blood that had recently fallen to the floor. He stepped up to the throne, his reddened gauze bandages sticking out in every direction.

"Why are you giving him anything?" said DiMachio gruffly.

"We structured Big's original contract so we retained the rights to his records forever, but superstar artists get control of their recordings after a certain number of years."

DiMachio drummed his fingers on his mobile throne armrest. "We invest the money up front. We own the masters; we're paying for them. Why should they get anything?"

"It's industry standard. We can't retain ownership forever, so we hold on as long as we can to make as much money as possible."

"Just say no," said DiMachio angrily as he glared at his senior executive. "They're ours."

Langley puffed nervously on the cigarette he'd forgotten was between his fingers. "Negotiations will stop. We have to grant reversion at some point."

DiMachio shot an evil glance at Bret Horowitz, e.l. Friend or no friend, personal lawyer or not, renegotiations were war. DiMachio knew master reversion issues were vital to a record company's profits. The lyrics and music of every song were controlled by the music publisher, so all the record company owned were the actual sound recordings of those songs that were laid down onto master tapes during the term of the artist's contract. The longer a record company owned the masters, the more royalties they earned from record sales.

Deity DiMachio looked back at Senior Senior Executive President of Business Affairs and Law, and General Counsel, Langley. "If you give in to that legal slime ball, make damn sure this company makes a lot of money first." DiMachio turned away from Langley and stared back down the conference room table.

Langley rushed back to his negotiating chair and lit up two more cigarettes, replacing the ones that had burned out.

The opposing side began another volley.

"Seven!" Bret Horowitz, entertainment lawyer, yelled.

"Twenty-five!" Langley yelled back in return, his nicotine-stained fingers trembling from battlefield adrenalin.

Bret Horowitz, e.l., rose to his feet and leaned on his hands while he bent forward over the table. "I said SEVEN!"

Langley rose to meet him, his eyes beginning to bulge. "Twenty-five, damn it!" he screamed in return.

Bret Horowitz, e.l., leaned further across the table. "Seven!" he screamed in Langley's face.

"Twenty-five!" volleyed back with equal intensity.

The two lawyers were nose to nose, screaming at the top of their lungs.

"Twenty-five!" "Seven!" "Twenty-five!" "Seven!" "Twenty-five!" "Seven!"

Langley clenched his fists and stomped his feet. "Twenty-five, Twenty-five, Twenty-five, damn it!"

DiMachio saw the warning signs and disappeared behind his throne. He peeked around the back of his chair, cautious, yet perversely curious.

"Seven, you low-life piece of corporate scum!"

Langley's eyes bulged as the veins in his neck pounded harder and harder against his battered, bruised, and sutured flesh. He clenched his fists tighter and stomped his feet harder in a childlike tantrum. "Twenty-five, twenty-five, twenty-five!" roared Langley in Bret Horowitz, e.l.'s, face.

"No, you pathetic piece of humanity! Seven!"

"TWENTY-FIVE!!" Langley erupted, a geyser of blood spewing forth from gaping neck fissures. The force of the explosion threw Bret Horowitz, entertainment lawyer, off balance. He fell backward into the conference room wall, temporarily blinded by the blood in his eyes. Reams of contract papers scattered crazily about the room, falling to the floor or sticking to the blood-stained conference room walls.

Langley grabbed his neck and fell back into his chair, frantically searching for his assistant shocker. He groped blindly around the table but couldn't find the control panel under the rubble of papers and blood. He reached under the meeting room table and hit the emergency buzzer his assistant Alex had installed two weeks earlier when he first began his major eruptions.

He pressed the button with his right hand while his left began to sink into the volcanic crater he had created in his neck.

*

Alex casually walked into the room, her red-stained yellow rubber boots squeaking through the bloody mess. She wore a disposable surgical gown and gloves, necessary attire after she realized most of her clothes had been stained beyond repair. Her medical bag was slung across her shoulder. She carried an IV pole in one hand and a gallon of blood in the other. A large floral shower cap protected and hid her hair. She stopped in front of Langley, an almost undetectable smirk on her face, and unzipped her medical bag.

"Hurry the hell up," Langley croaked as he sat covered in his own red, juicy blood, his hands desperately trying to pinch shut his ripped open flesh. Blood continued to pour out of his neck, down his shirt and pants, and into the pool of blood that had formed on the floor under his chair.

"Going as fast as I can," said Alex as she pulled out the IV equipment, taking leisurely care with all she did. She attached the plastic tube to the bag of blood and rammed the needle into his arm as hard as she could without permanently injuring him.

"Whoops, no good veins there," said Alex as she yanked the needle back out.

Langley's eyes rolled to the back of his head in semi-consciousness. A painful moan escaped his lips.

"We'll have to find a better spot," said Alex cheerfully as she moved down toward Langley's wrist. "Let's try here."

She shoved the needle into the fleshy part of his lower arm.

"No, that's no good either."

Alex slowly pulled out the needle so her boss could feel every excruciating second of the metal being removed from his skin. She felt a morbid sense of self-satisfaction as she watched Langley writhing in pain. She turned over his palm and looked at the back of his hand.

"There's only one place left to try." Alex took the three-inch-long needle and placed it on the back of her boss' hand.

"No, no, not there," Langley groaned.

"There's nowhere else," said Alex matter-of-factly, a small smirk still playing at the corners of her mouth. "You've been exploding so much we've used up all your other spots."

Alex slowly pushed the long needle into the back of her boss' hand, just under the flesh and above the bone.

The burn made Langley cry out in pain. Alex taped what little was left showing of the needle to the back of his hand. She hung the gallon of blood on the IV pole, stepping back to make sure everything was in the right position.

"I'm going to die if you don't hurry the hell up, you stupid, fat cow," Langley croaked.

Alex stepped back, her eyes alight with fiery rage. "What did you just call me?"

Langley clutched his neck and said nothing.

Alex leaned close to her boss, her face hard and full of hate, and hissed in his ear. "You ever talk to me like that again, you piece of shit, and I'll make sure you bleed to death."

She straightened up and pulled the suturing needle and thread from her medical repair bag. She knew it didn't matter how much she hurt him or what she said. Ever since the day she erupted and spoke back to him, he was different. Langley still yelled and exploded, but in a sick way he seemed to enjoy her abuse.

Alex pierced Langley's flesh and began sewing up the gaping hole with her patented Langley stitch, making sure she jabbed the needle in hard and yanked tightly on the suturing thread. She was sickened by the perverted mess she'd gotten herself into.

*

DiMachio peered around his mobile throne, mesmerized by the sight in front of him. Bret Horowitz, e.l., blinded by the blood splattered on his face, fumbled and groped for something to wipe away the ooze impairing his vision. The six supporting lawyers, three on each side of the table, were covered in blood, and a fresh coat of Langley oozed on the walls, table, and papers everywhere in the room. Bret Horowitz, e.l., grabbed a handful of papers from the table.

"Seven," said Bret Horowitz, e.l., as he wiped away the bloody slime with page twenty of Big's contract.

Langley feebly lifted his head and looked at Horowitz while Alex continued to sew up her boss' neck. "Twenty-five," Langley croaked in return.

DiMachio looked at Senior Senior Executive President of Business Affairs and Law, and General Counsel, Langley with what could almost be called respect. Langley might have screwed up Big's contract, but he was certainly laying his life on the line to get the best terms possible.

As DiMachio watched Langley struggle to stay conscious and continue the renegotiation, he realized Langley enjoyed the bloody battle. DiMachio came out from behind his throne and pressed a button under his left armrest. A wooden plank, his secretarial dictation seat, slid out from the side of his throne. No need to interrupt the meeting by having the housekeeping janitorial service come clean the bloody mess. This was better than boxing, better than sumo mud wrestling; it was almost like some seventies sex parties he'd been to.

Deity DiMachio sat on the piece of wood, mesmerized by the new sport he'd just discovered. He'd have to sit in on renegotiations more often.

Bret Horowitz, e.l., wrung Langley's blood out of his balding, yet pony tailed, hair. "I said seven."

"Twenty-five," said Senior Senior Executive President of Business Affairs and Law, and General Counsel, Langley as blood spurted from the remaining hole in his neck.

*

Alex finished sewing the special, over the top, modified X back stitch she had invented for sealing nasty Langley wounds, capping off the latest explosion of blood. She stood back and observed her handiwork, satisfied she had learned to prolong and enhance Langley's pain without actually killing him.

Alex saw a thick black floret of blood on Langley's neck. Her boss was coagulating and would be fine. She repacked her medical kit, checked to make sure the IV in Langley's hand was dripping blood at a steady rate and walked to the door.

As she walked by DiMachio, she turned around. "Sixteen," she said sarcastically to the room before disappearing out the door.

*

"Sixteen," said Deity DiMachio with executive authority.

The two lawyers stared at each other in silence. The only sound was the steady drip of Langley's blood as it drained to the floor from various pieces of furniture.

"Sixteen," said DiMachio again, his foot tapping impatiently as he glared at Langley.

The two lawyers continued to stare at each other across the table. Langley glanced in DiMachio's direction and saw the smug look of satisfaction on the Deity's face. Langley looked back at Horowitz and nodded almost imperceptibly.

Bret Horowitz, e.l., nodded briefly in return, setting off a chain reaction. Soon both lawyers were in front of each other, their heads bobbing up and down, smiles almost crossing their faces.

Corporate lawyers were soldiers, generals in the war of industrialization and big business. They skirmished over contracts; they sabotaged for the good of their corporation; they did anything to make as much money as possible, for themselves first, for the company they worked for second. They fought the battles of the twenty-first century.

The two lawyers shook hands. The renegotiation was over.

Fifteen

Alex raced inside the Acht monolith, her hair streaked ill green. She glanced quickly at her watch. Nine twenty-five. Twenty minutes before mandatory cerebrum urn check and five minutes before Secretary Security time check. And she was not in the mood to get written up and lectured by the mamby-assed Secretary Security Officers, a bunch of wannabe, ass-licking, corporate suck-ups who were trying to get promoted into an executive position, and who would do anything to get there, even sell their soul. What amazed Alex the most was the waiting list of people who wanted to be assigned to this military-type position.

She rushed past the regulatory control force hard at work screening and fingerprinting visitors. She hurried past the imposing floor to ceiling stone Grecian columns that lined the walls of the lobby and approached Checkpoint Vinny. She pulled out her ID badge and showed it to the armed security officer. She placed her hand on the security control panel and was permitted entrance once her fingerprints registered and the steel control gates rose.

Alex hurried over to the employee elevators and was dismayed to find a mob of people waiting. She looked at her watch again. Nine twenty-eight. If she was late one more time, the Secretary Security officers would have to inform Langley, more than enough reason for him to explode.

An elevator car opened its doors, and the mob pressed forward.

"I work for Langley; I have to get on," said Alex as she pushed her way to the front.

A unified murmur of sympathy floated through the air as her fellow employees stepped aside and allowed her entrance to the car.

"Thanks everyone," said Alex as she stepped on the elevator and tried to catch her breath. Mornings were usually bad, but this morning had been the worst. Alex had gotten up late, taken too many liberties with the snooze button, and had forgotten how much vodka she had consumed in front of the TV the night before.

When she slid her feet over the side of her bed and let them fall to the floor, Alex knew she was in trouble. Her heart pounded from the vodka, her lungs burned from too many cigarettes, and her abdomen churned and pinched several days earlier than it should have. Alex first vowed to stop the vodka, though she'd been making herself that promise for nearly a year. The alcohol relaxed her, the drunk helped her forget, but the hangovers had started making her feel like death. On those days, she spent most of her work time trying to stay alive, so one good thing she discovered was that her hangovers helped keep her mind off Langley.

Alex had rushed around her apartment, frantically getting ready for work. She showered, brushed her teeth, combed her hair, and threw on the clothes she had fortunately thought to leave out the night before. But as she hurried toward the front door of her small one-bedroom apartment, she felt gushing warmth between her legs. Alex cursed loudly, using every four-letter word she could think of as she ripped off all her clothes, hopped in the shower to clean herself off, and left her stained underwear and jeans to soak in cold water.

Alex didn't have to check the clock to know she was running far behind schedule, so she stacked three extra super absorbent maxi pads on top of each other and stuck them to her underwear. She threw on the first top she found but groaned when she realized her other pair of jeans wouldn't go over her bloated stomach and feminine protection bulge. Alex ripped off the pants and threw on a pair of leggings. She grabbed her backpack, yelled goodbye to her cat, and rushed out of her East Village apartment. Sunglasses in place, she walked to Broadway in a hung-over daze and took the subway to forty-ninth street, not thinking to look in her full-length mirror before she left.

Thirty-four elevator stops later, Alex was deposited on the executive floor. Hellie was already at her post, her mutant sea creatures swimming gaily in the fish tank, her Ticonderoga number two pencil tapping a Broadway show tune against the glass.

"Hi, Hellie," said Alex as she grabbed her timecard from the wall by reception.

"Don't worry about it, Alex," said Hellie as she turned around, a smile on her face.

"What?"

Hellie looked at Alex's timecard. "I said, don't worry about it."

Alex glanced down and saw she had already been punched in. "I owe you one, thanks," said Alex as she put her card back into its time slot. "But you don't have to. You know what can happen."

Hellie shrugged and tapped her eraser lightly against the glass, conducting her sea creatures in synchronized grace.

Alex walked down the hall and checked her watch again. Nine thirty-five. Ten minutes until the cerebrum patrol made their rounds. Any secretary caught with their brain in more than three times would be reported to the Cerebrum Security Council, with immediate termination a possibility. She entered her secretarial suite and unzipped the side of her head, pulling out her brain and placing it in her urn.

She sat in her chair, her wad of maxi pads and slippery flow making her feel unclean and uncomfortable, and prepared herself for another day of abuse and tedium.

The morning ankle shock made her forget her medical and hangover discomforts. The second jolt made Alex leap to her feet and head for the vending area, her hair streaked black, magenta, and green. She performed her daily Langley routine and fetched his coffee and packet of Twinkies, placing them on the designated spots on his desk.

"Shut the door," said Langley.

Alex loathed these closed-door meetings. It meant she had done something wrong, whether or not she actually had. Alex shut the door but left a two-inch crack for safety. She walked to her steno stool and sat down, her anger already raised in defense.

Langley slid an envelope across, and off, his desk. "What the hell is that?"

Alex leaned over and picked the envelope from the floor. She turned it over and saw it was addressed to her.

"An envelope addressed to me."

Langley began to shake. "I know that you imbecile. Why do you have one?"

127

Alex opened the flap and pulled out a company invitation to Big's party, to be held at the Starshine Ballroom in two weeks.

"I guess because I've been invited to the party."

"That's not what I asked!"

Langley stood and pounded the desk with his fist. "How many times do I have to tell you to focus on my exact words, not your interpretation of them. I asked you what the envelope was. *That* is the question I want answered." Langley pounded the desk again. "Focus and precision are necessary in this job. You need to learn to listen and to think!"

Alex looked at Langley, her hangover gone and her hair becoming blacker by the second. "How can I think if I'm not allowed to have a brain?"

Langley's face and neck turned purple as his head and body began to shake uncontrollably. He pounded both fists on his desk while he yelled.

"This is not a democracy! You are here to cater to MY moods and personality, not vice versa. You are not here to ask questions; you are here to answer them! I'm going to ask you one more time. What is that envelope?"

Alex couldn't control the anger that seeped into her voice. "It's an invitation to Big's party. And if you'd read the memo sent out last week, you'd know every employee of this company is invited to Big's party. Even me!"

Langley's eyes bulged from his head. "I don't believe you. I never saw any memo." He leaned across his desk, his face full of hate. "Did you sleep with someone?" He leaned even closer to Alex. "Did you *fuck* someone to get yourself invited?"

Alex stood up and headed for the door. "I don't have to subject myself to this. It's my invitation; I got invited."

Langley scurried around from behind his desk, his entire body purple and shaking, his eyes popping out six inches from his face. "Don't you walk out on me; don't you dare walk out of this room! So help me god, you'll regret it."

Alex stopped in her tracks and turned around, her anger threatening to overpower her. "What, Langley, what are you going to do? Explode on me? Drench me with your blood?" She shook with anger. "Go ahead, blow all you want."

Langley clenched both his fists and stomped up and down. "Listen to me; listen to me; listen to me! I'm in charge here!" He stomped his feet and shook until his body couldn't take the pressure. He exploded, shooting blood across the office.

Alex looked at him, his hate now filling her eyes. "Go suture yourself, Langley. I've had it with the bad mouthing, the threats, the explosions."

She opened the door and walked out as her boss clutched his neck and bled.

Alex performed her routine morning duties with pockets full of candy and an anger that ate at her stomach.

She yanked papers from the fax machine and threw them on top of the mail. She grabbed a pile of interoffice memos from her desk and stormed toward Langley's office.

She stopped at the doorway, her mouth dropping open in shock. There, in front of her, in the reflection of the glass-framed poster on the inner office wall, was her boss, his neck crazily wrapped with white surgical gauze, sliding a whole Twinkie in and out of his mouth. He was giving a blow job to a piece of junk food.

Alex leaned her head back and screamed a silent scream of disgust, her shock making her momentarily forget her anger. She could hear Langley's desk chair rhythmically sliding back and forth as sucking sounds started to fill the air. She saw him shove his tongue in one end of the sponge cake and start thrusting it in and out of the white cream center. Alex jumped as she felt something behind her. She quickly turned and put her finger over her mouth.

Clef zipped up next to her and silently handed her a cassette. He was dressed in fishing gear from head to toe, including a rain hat covered in fishing lures. Normally, Alex would try to guess the name of the band before looking at the cassette, but she simply couldn't take her eyes off Langley's reflection. Clef followed her gaze and jumped in horror.

"Oh, my," was all that quietly squeaked from his lips. Alex watched the Roadrunner of Rock turn on his heel and zip down the hall, his British awkwardness at any sign of emotion apparent in his steps.

When she turned back to the poster reflection, she saw Langley shoving the Twinkie awkwardly into his mouth. He must have seen or heard them standing there. Alex entered the office quickly and avoided Langley's glare and the noises he was making as he tried to swallow the dry sponge-like cake. She shoved the mail into his inbox and removed the papers sitting in his outbox.

Alex rushed out of his office and ran into the fire escape stairwell. A huge scream of disgust shot out of her mouth but was quickly replaced by a piece of chocolate. She then continued to photocopy and sort, highlighting the various recipients and cc's on the notes and memos Langley had written. She ran the floors of Acht, hand delivering each piece of paper and trying to erase the image stuck in her head.

She returned to the executive floor and rushed by Hellie, grabbing Langley's phone messages. When she returned to her desk, she saw a note to Jiglio on her chair. "Status of Big at radio. Anything to discuss?" Alex made her mandatory three copies, one for the central Big file, one for Langley's personal Big file and one for her own chronological file, and ran to Jiglio's office. She dropped off the note and returned, only to find another stack of memos and notes on her chair. She copied, delivered, and returned to her desk exhausted. She popped a couple ibuprofen pills in her mouth and swallowed them with water. She followed them with a handful of M&M's.

"Alex, empty my outbox!"

Alex's hair streaked its familiar looking black and magenta, but mixed with the ill green from her period. She stood and went into Langley's office, handing him his phone messages and retrieving two pieces of paper from his box. She made more copies and hand delivered the notes asking two of the vice presidents of law out to lunch. When she returned to her chair, she saw yet another piece of paper of no importance to the same two lawyers she had just delivered to.

"That's it," said Alex and sat down. She shoved the piece of paper into her delivery folder.

"Alex, my box!"

Alex went into his office and pulled one piece of paper from his out box. She made her mandatory copies of both papers and delivered them to the appropriate people.

When she came back to her secretarial suite, she saw another note from Langley on her chair, this time addressed to her. "A. You are spending far too much time away from your desk. No excuses. You work for me. If this doesn't stop, disciplinary action will be taken."

Alex's hair turned jet black as she ate another piece of candy. He was obviously getting back at her for letting him bleed earlier, and for the scene she'd witnessed with the Twinkie.

She stamped more mail and took the papers into Langley's office. Another note sat in his out box. She grabbed the note, made copies, and rushed down the hall to Derby's office.

She entered his outer office, the secretarial suite his secretary should have been in but wasn't because Derby couldn't keep a secretary. They all mysteriously quit within six months of being hired. When Alex dropped the note in his mail tray, she felt a presence behind her, eyes boring through her back. She turned and saw Derby crouched next to a large black leather waiting room chair, his ornate silver fork trembling excitedly behind his ear while sweat ran down the side of his face. His eyes were glued to Alex's leggings.

Alex momentarily froze as she felt Derby's heat grow more and more intense. She turned away in disgust and returned to her desk, only to find two more notes on her chair. Langley was obviously out for revenge. And rather than fire her, he seemed to like this type of abuse much more.

Alex made her required three copies and copies for everyone on the distribution list, and stormed down the halls one more time. When she entered Derby's office, she again felt his eyes. She glanced to her right and saw him standing behind a six-foot potted plant, his airline food, mini bar stuffed, fat stomach bulging through the leaves. His two lower shirt buttons had popped open; long black hairs broke through and curled among the plant leaves. Alex put Langley's note in Derby's mail tray, ignoring the rustling of the plant leaves, and hurried down the hall to finish her deliveries.

When Alex finished her latest delivery round, she headed back to her secretarial suite. She rushed down the hall but stopped when she saw Derby standing in the middle of the hallway, blocking her path. Alex

131

could see his eyes were still glued between her legs. She lowered her head and tried to rush by the Senior Senior Executive President of Sales and Marketing.

A clammy hand reached out and stopped her. "You work for Langley, right?" asked Derby.

"Yes," said Alex gruffly as she felt his sweat seep through her shirt and onto her skin.

"What's your name?"

"Alex," she said as she squirmed out from under his grasp.

"Good," said Derby, his eyes still fixed on her legs.

Alex broke free and hurried to the bathroom. When she looked in the floor to ceiling mirror, she was horrified. In her crazed rush that morning, Alex hadn't looked in the mirror, so she didn't realize the three bulky maxi pads she was wearing had created a penis-type bulge. And because she had accidentally put on a sweater that stopped just short of her abdomen, her bulge was obvious to anyone who looked.

Alex walked back to her desk. She felt oddly confused yet strangely curious at Derby's sudden interest in her. He'd never said so much as hello in the year plus Alex had been at the company, so why the sudden interest? She entered her suite and saw another mountain of paper on her chair. She reflexively copied, highlighted and delivered, running back and forth between different floors and her secretarial suite.

Late in the afternoon, Alex fell into her chair, exhausted from her secretarial work out.

"Alex, get in here and shut the door!"

Alex glanced at her cerebrum urn, too tired to say anything. Her brain floated in its juice, silent and uncommunicative. She sighed and stood up. Alex walked into Langley's room and shut the door for the second time that day, wondering what had happened this time. She sat on her steno stool, too tired from running and too exhausted from cramps to care that he might explode. She flipped back her stressed magenta and ill green streaked hair and looked him squarely in the eye.

Langley had three cigarettes burning in the ashtray, the smoke creating a protective shroud. He stared back at her, but his eyes kept glancing at her lap and the bulge protruding from her leggings.

Langley cleared his throat. He was smoking two cigarettes at once, his lungs barely able to absorb oxygen. His attitude was ambivalent, as opposed to his usual inflexible bullheadedness.

"Derby just phoned."

"Oh," was the only reply Alex could muster.

"Seems he noticed your future potential," said Langley as his eyes searched his desktop, most likely looking for Twinkie crumbs from that morning. "Seems he liked what he saw."

Alex saw Langley glance at her vaginal area. She remained silent for several seconds, not comprehending Langley's words. She finally spoke, uttering the only comment floating through her brainless cranium.

"I don't understand."

"Go put your brain in," said Langley.

"But I can't," said Alex with genuine surprise. "It's not six yet."

Langley lit another cigarette, replacing one of the three previous smoke sticks that had burned out. He took a deep breath, inhaling his own secondhand smoke, and remained eerily calm for a man who was prone to bodily explosions at the mere hint of noncompliance.

"If I tell you to put your brain in, put your brain in." He stared at Alex, his face hard but for the first time not violent. "Do as I say."

Alex stood and walked to her desk, guilty for disobeying company policy, yet feeling liberated. She unzipped the side of her head and pulled her brain out of her Acht cerebrum urn. Her brain stem wiggled a little greeting.

When Alex returned to Langley's office, fully alert and cognizant for the first time, she nearly laughed out loud. Langley was no longer the evil monster that had controlled her life for so long; instead, he appeared small, pathetic, and inconsequential, a shadow of a human being. Alex couldn't believe someone as insignificant as Langley had tyrannized and dominated her for so long. She walked past her steno stool and sat down in the guest chair on the other side of his desk, her maxi pads bunching up on her abdomen.

Alex watched, both confused and amused, as her boss groped for words.

Langley coughed nervously. "So, as I said, Derby was impressed with you and your future potential here at the company."

He lit another cigarette. "Derby phoned DiMachio and got approval to promote you to product manager."

"Excuse me?" said Alex with genuine shock.

Langley fidgeted in his chair as he practically ate his cigarettes. "I said you've been promoted to product manager."

Alex leaned forward in her chair, still not fully comprehending. "I'm getting a promotion?"

Langley nodded, his eyes avoiding hers.

Alex sat back flabbergasted. After almost two years interviewing for jobs that were already filled, of meetings with executives who were as crazy or crazier than Langley, of countless rejections, and after giving up hope of getting anywhere in the company, Alex was being offered a mid-level management position. It was an offer unheard of in a major record company, unless, of course, you were male or knew the right people at the top.

Alex continued to stare at Langley, trying to let his words sink in, but it was too preposterous for her to fully comprehend. It was so ridiculous, she felt like laughing out loud. Langley continued talking but she found it hard to concentrate on anything he was saying.

"You can't fraternize with brainless personnel, unless you want to sleep with them," said Langley. "Remember that, especially when you start hiring people. Everyone in this company has a place, a role. They were established long before us, and they'll be here long after we're gone. So, while we're here, it's our job to uphold and respect them."

Alex looked at her blood and nicotine encrusted boss and almost heard what he was saying, but she was still too shocked over her sudden promotion to fully comprehend his words. He droned on about company policy and the way the organization operated; Alex watched as the hollow words fell meaninglessly from Langley's mouth.

She leaned back in the guest chair, her muscles starting to relax after her extended physical workout earlier in the day. Her mouth slowly opened, stretching to its limit. She closed her eyes and reflexively put her hand to her mouth as she let out a satisfied 'ahh' and a rush of air.

Alex sat up startled and looked at Langley. She had never yawned in his face before. He stopped droning and took a long drag off his two lit cigarettes. He remained silent but stood up, and for the first time since Alex started working for him, he held out his hand. She hesitated for only a second, then stood and confidently returned the gesture, shaking the limp hand outstretched in front of her. She saw Langley's eyes grow larger when he glanced between her legs.

Alex walked out of his office confused. She had always thought this would be her moment of revenge, her time to make Langley pay for all the pain he had put her through. Alex had spent many nights fantasizing about her day of liberation and what she would say and do to her boss when he became her former employer, but rather than being ecstatic over her long-awaited freedom, an unsettling cloud of apprehension overshadowed any joy she felt.

Sixteen

On the day it all began to unravel, Skeater was at his desk at nine-thirty, his two cans of Tab breakfast in front of him and nearly gone. He looked over his mountain of printed emails and memos, unsure of where to begin. The A&R music man had memos to read, memos to return replying to the memos he'd read, memos to write regarding the memos he'd read and replied to, and sometimes he had to write memos about writing memos. The memos then generated meetings so executives could discuss the memos face to face, resulting in more memos clarifying and revising earlier memos, often with prior memos attached, which in turn created more meetings and more memos.

And in between all the memos and meetings were the phone calls. Most phone calls were return calls, responses to earlier calls that oftentimes were a response to an even earlier call or an even earlier, earlier call. Phone messages piled up so high during the day that many times both parties forgot what the initial call was regarding and who originally placed it.

Skeater unplugged his phone and stuck his hand into the mountain of paper on his desk, pulling out a pile of memos. He picked up his pen and began attacking the monster page by page.

The first memo was from one of the six vice presidents of A&R under him. 'Skeat, Farfalle have gone over budget in the studio. We need $$. At least twenty thousand. Viper.'

Skeater jotted a 'yes' in thick red marker and made a note to look into the vice president's overall spending habits.

The second memo was a request from one of the talent scouts to up the bidding amount for a hot, new, hip band that, according to the scout, 'everyone was trying to sign'. Skeater scribbled a 'see me to discuss'. Many times, A&R people lost sight of the fact that bands 'everyone' wanted became more desirable, and therefore more valuable, because of the bidding war, not because of the music.

The next piece of paper was a letter from the manager of an unsigned band, following up on a demo tape she had submitted several months earlier. Unlike most of his peers, Skeater accepted unsolicited tapes, tapes from anyone, rather than demos submitted by other people in the music industry.

The A&R executive turned around and looked at the six-foot-plus high mountain behind him. Hundreds of manila envelopes, white envelopes, padded jiffy bags and boxes of all shapes and sizes were stacked against his wall rising well above his head. Each had been logged in and labeled by his assistant, Juanita, but the usually alphabetized orderly stack had turned into an overgrown and disorganized jungle of mail. Skeater had even removed the surgically implanted headphones from his ears; these days, he didn't have spare time to listen to music.

Skeater sighed with despair. He was doing three times more work than he was three years ago when he first got promoted; his administrative duties had increased in proportion to the amount of time he worked as the head of A&R. Skeater had even started coming to work earlier and earlier, hoping he could catch up on his paperwork and get back to doing what he loved most - listening to new music.

Skeater stared at the wall of envelopes, knowing it was no use; he would never find the band's tape. He reluctantly reached up and placed the letter on the pile of envelopes. What saddened Skeater was the realization he might never be able to search for new bands again, the one thing he had always loved.

He turned back to his desk, his shoulders sagging, his head down. When Skeater looked up, his stacks of paper had each risen to over three feet. He took off his aviator sunglasses and rubbed his eyes, wondering how he would ever reply to and comment on all the words surrounding him.

When Skeater opened his eyes, he saw the legs of his assistant walking through the door. The rest of her body was hidden behind another column of memos and letters, a column that teetered precariously with each step she took.

"Juanita," said Skeater after his assistant had safely placed the papers on his desk, making the piles so high Skeater could no longer see over them. "Juanita, how much more mail is there?"

"Lots," floated over the wall of white.

Juanita left Skeater to tackle the walls of his fortress. He was completely hidden, with three-foot stacks of paper boxing him in on three sides. He randomly chose whatever was on top; prioritizing had become impossible. Skeater lost himself in corporate haggling and re-haggling, trying to sort out his department's difficulties and dilemmas with the least amount of involvement or refereeing possible. An hour passed with the A&R man trying to put a dent in his stacks, yet the more Skeater tried to get through his paperwork, the more the papers rose on his desk.

The Senior Senior Executive President of A&R reached over for his between-meal snack treat of Tab that Juanita at some point had kindly put in front of him. As he picked up the hot pink can and brought it toward his mouth, he watched in detached horror as the full can of soda slipped through his fingers. It fell onto his recycled desk blotter, the carbonated syrup soaked up by the reams of paper surrounding him.

Skeater massaged his left arm, but it had no feeling. Heart attack was his first thought. He stood in a panic and stumbled through the papers covering his desk and floor, making his way to the men's room.

He entered the linoleum-tiled sanctuary and threw cold water on his face. He took slow, controlled breaths as he raised his arm in the air, trying to get blood flowing back through his veins. Skeater looked up and was shocked at what stared back at him in the mirror, a man who had aged ten years in less than one, who once emanated teen heart throb energy and now resembled a corpse. Grey hairs peeked out on his temples, giving his shag hair cut more of a dirty mop feel. Skeater's eyes were sunken and hollow, with dark, purple raccoon circles. His skin was a permanent ashen gray, from too little sun, too much Tab, and not enough vitamins.

Skeater turned away from the mirror, not wanting to witness any more of his self-decay. He entered a stall and sat fully clothed on the toilet throne, the door open. The bathroom was one of the few places a man could contemplate his life in peace, and Skeater needed a little time to himself. He continued to massage his arm and sighed with relief when the tingling pins and needles sensation ran through his limb, signaling the return of normal blood flow.

Skeater knew he was fortunate, knew he'd been able to do almost everything he'd ever wanted. He had always loved music; it made him feel connected to the world. He played in a band in his teens, went to thousands of concerts over his life, and, somehow, he miraculously ended up being paid a salary for simply doing what he loved to do. He had traveled the world in his pursuit of music, had been exposed to other people and other cultures he never knew existed. He had met and befriended some of the great artists of the twentieth century and had lived a fairy tale life of glamor and fame while never having to suffer its trappings.

The men's room door swung open. A figure zipped over to the urinal, did his business, shook, and was done in a startling-fast five seconds. He emitted his trademark short, dry cough and spun around to exit the room and return to pushing his bands to the clogged arteries of the corporate machine.

"Skeater," said a surprised Clef as he spotted the A&R executive on the toilet.

The Roadrunner of Rock rushed forward, his arms and legs flailing about with his usual repressed energy and overall hyperactivity, and shook hands with the Skeater. "How's it going, eh?"

Skeater looked at Clef. "Alright, I guess; I'm under a lot of pressure these days."

"Pressure, yes, pressure. I know pressure," said Clef as he fidgeted with all parts of his body. "Bands want this, record companies want that; I'm trying to please both."

Clef opened his thick black, imitation fur knapsack. It wasn't until Skeater saw the backpack that he noticed Clef's outfit. The owner of Black Dog Records, a subsidiary of Acht, stood before Skeater in a uniform of red and black. On his head rested a two-foot high, rounded hat of long, thick fake black fur. The hat rested on his head like a grossly oversized Beatles wig, with imitation black animal hair reaching down into his eyes and hiding all but the lower portion of his face. An inch thick band of gold brocade looped across his face, the space between his chin and lower lip stopping the royal strap from snapping into his nose or eyes. His pants were royal regulation black with a red stripe on each of the outer legs, and his military-looking jacket was fire-engine red with gold collar and cuff trim, and eight white buttons ran down the front.

"The Guards," said Skeater before Clef handed him a tape.

"Close," answered Clef. "Changing of the Guard."

The Roadrunner of Rock handed a cassette to Skeater.

Skeater remained on the toilet seat. "Clef, can I ask you something?"

Arms flailed, nervousness mounted, but Clef said, "Sure."

"What do you want out of all this?"

"All what?"

Skeater opened his arms. "All this. The music, the business. Rock and roll. What do you want out of it?"

Clef nearly bounced off the walls. "Don't really know what you're asking. This is all there is. I've got the bands. I'm traveling. I'm lucky; I get to sign most music I want. I'm doing what I want. Can't ask for more."

"But," said Skeater. "What if the music, the bands, everything, was gone tomorrow? What would you have? What would it be worth?"

Clef emitted a short, dry cough.

"Don't know, don't know," he said to the ground, a momentary gray cloud of dread passing through his eyes. The Indie Kingpin and Roadrunner of Rock regained his reserved, unemotional British composure and looked at Skeater. "Why worry about it? There'll always be another band, always more music. It'll never go away."

Clef closed his backpack and adjusted his two-foot high, fake fur, Queen's Guard helmet. "Gotta run. Got music to get to the masses."

The two men shook hands. Clef disappeared out the door before Skeater had time to lower his arm.

Skeater came to work at eight the next morning, determined to get through his paperwork and to approach each day with a more positive, relaxed attitude. As he rounded the corner to the lower-level elevator bank, his pet ferret tucked comfortably under his arm, he spotted Alex standing alone, her hair streaked stress magenta and flowing wildly about her.

"You're here awfully early," said Skeater as he approached her, his heart pounding.

The stress was obvious in more than Alex's hair as she nervously fidgeted with her coat buttons.

140

"It's my new job," said Alex as she glanced in Skeater's direction. "I got promoted to Product Manager, and it seems the main difference between this and working for Langley is now I have dozens of people screaming at me instead of one."

Skeater smiled warmly. "You get used to it; you learn to tune a lot of it out." He unconsciously stepped closer to Alex. "How long have you been at the job?"

Alex paused for a second, then replied. "It seems like forever, but it's only been a couple months."

The elevator bell rang. Skeater bowed with a flourish to allow Alex on first.

"Thank you," she said as she stepped in, the purple strands sprinkling throughout her hair.

They pushed their respective floor buttons and ascended into the monolith, neither yet able to admit it, but both secretly hoping the ride would never end. Skeater's palms grew sweaty and his heart beat faster as he felt Alex's warmth surround him. He breathed in deeply and smelled her presence, a clean wholesomeness slightly scented with a fragrant perfume.

Skeater leaned back against the elevator wall, a warm smile again spreading across his face. "By the way, congratulations on the promotion. I'm a little behind on my paperwork, so I didn't see the announcement."

Alex blushed and lowered her head, smiling with humility and embarrassment. "Thanks. I still can't believe it."

Skeater looked at her quizzically. "Believe what, that you got promoted?"

Alex blushed with an even deeper shade of red. "Well, yeah. I spent so many years trying, it's hard to believe I'm finally a product manager." She looked at Skeater briefly and sheepishly shrugged her shoulders. "It's all so new. And weird."

Skeater shifted Skat to a more comfortable position under his arm and petted his stuffed fur. "Why weird?"

Alex shifted her weight from one foot to the other while the purple strands multiplied in her hair. "I don't know, it's hard to explain. I tried for so many years to get here and now that I've made it, I have to reevaluate myself. All the energy I put into getting that goal has to be redirected somewhere."

Skeater nodded with understanding.

Alex shook her head and looked at Skeater, smiling shyly. "I don't know what I'm talking about. It's too early for me to philosophize."

Skeater smiled as the bell rang, signaling his arrival on the twenty-third floor. "I think I understand what you mean." He reached out and gently patted Alex's arm. "Feel free to come down and philosophize any time you want." Skeater stepped out into the hallway. He looked back in the car and gave Alex a small wave. "See ya."

Alex raised her hand and returned the gesture. "See ya."

*

Alex rushed into her office, her entire body on fire from Skeater's touch. Had he really meant what he said, did he really want her to stop by his office, or was he just being nice and kissing her butt like so many other people were since they'd heard she'd been promoted to product manager?

Alex ran her fingers through her purple streaked, stress magenta hair. She smiled as she pictured the A&R man and his stuffed ferret. She was beginning to think she liked him more than she realized.

The phone interrupted her thoughts.

Alex picked up the receiver out of habit and awkwardness at having her own assistant. "Alex speaking."

"Where's the artwork for Splotch? It's not here! If I can't approve the proofs on time and this record's delayed, I'll phone Derby. I don't want to drop names and pull rank, but I'll have no choice but to tell him the record was delayed because of you..."

Alex held the phone away from her ear as the manager on the other end ranted and raved. As the bellowing continued, Alex checked her files, taking note of the fact that the artwork had been Federal Expressed the evening before.

When the verbal rampage slowed down, Alex cut in. "Have you gotten your Federal Express delivery this morning?"

"Federal Express delivery? What Federal Express delivery? Don't start blaming Federal Express."

Alex heard a click and realized she'd been put on hold. Several minutes later, the manager came back on the other end. "You're lucky the artwork just arrived; otherwise, I would've gone over your head."

The phone went dead. Alex pulled the receiver away from her ear and stared at it as a huge sigh escaped her mouth. She hung up the phone and reflexively opened her desk drawer, pulling out the honey coated raisin and graham clusters she had recently taken to munching on. She popped several granola bits in her mouth as her phone began ringing again.

Alex had started coming to work at eight in the morning so she could have one to two hours of uninterrupted work time, but it seemed her phone rang all hours of the day and night. So far Alex's job had consisted of putting out fires created by the product manager before her as well as the departments around her, and as each day passed, Alex began to realize that was her job. She was responsible for dealing with last-minute emergencies that had become last-minute emergencies due to previous emergencies that had taken up her time, forcing her to postpone daily responsibilities until they became last-minute emergencies. Day after day, emergency after emergency, Alex tried to get on top of her workload, but she found it impossible. There was too much work for one person.

When Alex had mentioned her dilemma to another product manager, he simply shrugged his shoulders in mock sympathy. "Sink or swim," were his words of advice, though he failed to mention the key to being overburdened was to always act overworked, even when not busy, to adopt a constant crazed look, and to pass as much work as possible to other people.

The ring of the phone caught Alex's attention. "Alex speaking."

"A&R told me Brunt's record is pushed back a month. You told me it would be out this month. What's going on?"

Alex fingered another granola cluster. "Hi Buddy. I don't know. When the A&R people get in, I'll find out."

"As soon as they're in. Everything's in place for this month."

Alex jotted a note on her already overflowing To Do list. "I promise. I'll get back to you."

Alex hung up the telephone and popped the piece of granola into her mouth as her hair streaked more magenta. When the phone started ringing again, she let it go to voicemail, knowing it was another crisis in someone else's eyes.

Alex read over her sorely neglected 'To Do' list. An advertising form had to be typed for three of her artists, in triplicate, and distributed to no less than fifteen people. A DNA genetic detector scan had to be scheduled so the finance department could project her lifespan, adjust her future salary accordingly, and monetarily prepare for any serious medical conditions that might occur in the years to come. A promo showcase tour had to be set up, a check requisition was needed for tour support; liner notes needed to be finalized on the *Babes of the 80's* compilation record; sticker request forms had to be circulated for an upcoming single, filled out in triplicate and distributed to ten people; a marketing plan had to be written, as well as a financial plan; an audio package needed to be ordered for an upcoming video to be shot in a week; a director and producer had to be found for another video; artwork had to be approved for two album covers.

And on top of all that, Alex had to schedule a week out of the office to attend a mandatory management training seminar. Topics included 'How to Get the Most Out of Your Secretary While Giving Her the Least Possible,' 'Getting Your Way Without Having a Tantrum,' and the ever-popular 'How to Make Money, Not Music.' Her list went on for two pages.

Alex attacked her work methodically, beginning with the first item on her 'To Do' list and painstakingly working through each task in front of her. She lost track of time as she typed up forms, made phone calls, and pushed mountains of paper around her permanently cluttered desk. Alex looked up with surprise when she heard her assistant Vernique rummaging around her desk.

"Can't believe she'd get here early," Alex muttered. She was shocked when her watch displayed ten twenty-five; two hours had passed as quickly as ten minutes, but there was no surprise that her assistant was twenty-five minutes late.

There was nothing Alex could do about her lack of help. Vernique had come with the job; her well-connected parents had befriended the Head Yakadan, thus ensuring their daughter a place at the company. Naturally, Vernique was exempt from security checks and the Cerebrum Extraction Procedure, though the CEP wasn't necessary for her assistant; she had so little to begin with.

"Vernique," Alex called out from her office. "Would you please empty my outbox and type some forms for me?"

The twenty-two-year-old, recent college graduate sighed loudly and leisurely got up from her desk. Her eyes were shallow and vacant, the eyes of someone who knew nothing of struggling, self-achievement or self-satisfaction. She walked into Alex's office, her new Donna Karan pant suit perfectly in tune with her body movements, her short, platinum blonde, cropped hair perfectly in place. Vernique reluctantly pulled the papers out of the box, her freshly manicured nails glistening with perfection, and returned to her desk to begin a hit and miss attempt at typing the forms into the computer. Typing was not one of Vernique's strong points, and Alex would have to retype most of them herself.

Alex realized early in her employment at Acht that a large part of the corporate game was learning to work around other people's deficiencies and incompetence, and in her new job she was learning how not to let other people's inadequacies reflect badly upon her.

Alex glanced at her watch and moaned. "Oh, god, the scheduling meeting."

She gathered her papers, grabbed her notebook and pen, and headed down the hall to one of the many mandatory meetings she had to attend each week, meetings that were necessary but cut into her workday and gave her little free time, except to answer the dozens of phone messages that would inevitably be stacked on her desk when she returned to her office before heading off to another meeting.

Alex entered the conference room and walked over to the far wall, glancing through one of the six-inch strips of window onto a city of concrete and corporate mentalities. The benefits, the supposed security, the medication when the human spirit rose above and fought the oppression was all a concerted effort, a way to keep the masses subservient and working hard so the minority ruling class could remain in power, their factories and businesses making money because of the hard work of their employees, the oppressed majority.

Something began to gnaw at Alex's psyche, something that troubled her and made her uneasy. Ever since Alex had started keeping her brain in, she'd had an uncomfortable feeling, like something wasn't quite right. She first thought her brain was readjusting to being back in her skull full time, but it was more than that. Alex's brain no longer tried speaking with her like it had when it was trapped in the Acht cerebrum urn. Instead, she could feel it festering inside her, plotting and scheming, waiting for an opportunity to teach her a lesson. Alex didn't understand what was happening, but as she looked out the window strip across Manhattan, she felt a seed that had been planted deep within her sprout and begin to grow.

*

Twelve floors below Alex, Skeater battled his own corporate demons. He sat at his desk, a cold can of Tab in front of him, and stared at the stacks of paper piled all over his office. He wondered how he'd gotten to this point in his life. Music was his passion - listening to it, discovering it, bringing great sounds to other people, but it seemed as if his life now consisted of paperwork, meetings, and shoving manufactured music down the throats of the public.

Skeater reached into the mountain before him and grabbed a stack of memos. He picked up his pen, looked briefly at Skat, and mechanically went to work.

"And this is success?" said Skeater aloud to himself and Skat as he wrote 'yes', 'no', 'absolutely not!', 'see me to discuss', and other assorted commands, answers, and questions on the papers before him. He looked behind him at the hundreds of tapes begging to be listened to, knowing it would be weeks before he could get to them, if he would ever be able to get to them at all.

When he turned back to his work, Skeater looked around in shock. His assistant Juanita wasn't at work yet, but he could have sworn his mound of papers had multiplied and nearly doubled in size in the several seconds he had taken his eyes off his desk. He instinctively picked Skat off the floor and placed the animal in front of him on the only free space on his desk. Skeater absentmindedly stroked his pet's fur as he read through note after note, memo after memo, trying to beat the paper that seemed intent on engulfing him.

His A&R staff wanted more money for bands, more money to complete albums, money for demo deals, money for touring. Everything was money, money, money. Skeater pushed up his Starsky sunglasses and rubbed his eyes, trying to figure out where all the money would come from. He looked back at the memos in front of him, but a cold, numbing sensation came over him.

146

His breath began to come in short gasps, and he realized with horror that his left leg had gone dead. Skeater pounded on his thigh, desperately trying to get the blood flowing, but his leg remained paralyzed. He didn't have time to sit in the bathroom, there were far too many memos surrounding him, and he had to get through them, had to make a dent, had to get something done so he might get five minutes to listen to music. He lost track of time as he forced himself to stay conscious and plow through his stacks.

By noon the papers had grown into piles over six feet high, surrounding him and blocking his desk. Skeater's breath became shallower as he struggled to keep up with all the paper. His Tab was gone, his mouth was dry, but he had to get through the paperwork. He had to keep going. By three o'clock, Skeater looked in horror around him. He was now completely engulfed in paper, with no way out. The stacks had grown so high, they nearly touched the ceiling; they had grown so wide, they had buried him in a coffin of paper. Skeater felt the numbness creep up his left side, partially paralyzing him from head to toe. He tried to move his mouth, to utter a cry for help, but nothing came out. He tried to stand but teetered off balance and fell back in his chair. He was buried, buried alive and all alone.

Skeater picked up Skat with his still functioning right hand and cuddled him close to his body. His breath came in shorter and shorter gasps as the room began to spin crazily around him. He remembered the sensation of sinking, of going down, down, down, into darkened depths of nothingness, away from the paperwork, away from the stress, away from everything around him. He sank faster and faster until he was falling, careening downward, further and further into the blackness. He felt his heartbeat quicken, the only sound as it pounded furiously in his ears. He saw nothing but black - cold, empty, sightless black - as he fell further and further into the void.

Terror ripped through Skeater's mind as he sensed something racing toward him, something big, something heavy, something that could end his life. It sped closer and closer, hurling itself at him with angry force. Skeater struggled and flailed but couldn't stop it. Just as he sensed it, knew it was close, he jerked his whole body and woke up in his seat.

He gasped for air as he looked around his darkened office. He was trapped in a corporate womb, the inner belly of a paper pushing machine. He must have passed out because everything was silent, everything was dark. Even the light had gone from his six-inch-wide window strips.

Skeater felt his chest tighten with pain as the right side of his body began to lose feeling. He panicked, knowing he had to do something before his entire body went numb. Skeater stood on his right leg and hopped from behind his desk, his pet Skat tucked firmly under his good arm. He threw himself into the fortress of papers, only to be thrown back onto the floor. He picked himself up, dazed but determined to get out alive. The A&R music man hopped back over to the wall of white that encircled him and again threw himself against the paper prison. The walls remained impenetrable.

Panicking, Skeater hopped back behind his desk and scrambled on top, his right side becoming as numb as his left. He stood and held Skat in front of his face to protect him from possible paper cuts. He took what could have been his last breath and threw himself up and against the white pulp wall. Skeater fell back onto his desk, panting heavily.

When he got back up on his one good, yet rapidly deteriorating, foot, he looked above him and noticed the papers toward the top had moved. Skeater grabbed Skat by his stuffed backside and pounded the papers with the wooden plaque the ferret was mounted on. He swung with all his might, pushing, pounding, and hitting until, finally, a few of the papers fell away.

Skeater shoved Skat under his paralyzed left arm. With his right hand he pushed at the papers above him, throwing himself at the mound until he felt it move ever so slightly. He grabbed a stack of papers from above and placed them on his desk, making a footstool for himself to climb on. He hopped onto the stack and reached the opening just above his head. The A&R executive clawed and dug at the wall until he could hoist himself and his only true friend up to the opening. Skeater shoved his head through the hole and pushed with Herculean might. The white fortress slowly teetered as papers began cascading down toward the ground.

Skeater let out a scream as he and Skat toppled with the wall. They slid over thousands of pieces of paper and belly surfed down the mountain of pulp and into the hall. He grabbed Skat with his good hand and scrambled for safety as papers began careening down around him, threatening to bury them alive. Skeater hopped and hobbled as fast as he could as a tidal wave of paper followed them down toward the elevator. The last thing the Senior Senior Executive President of A&R remembered was throwing Skat and himself into the elevator, knowing they had finally escaped.

Seventeen

It was the most coveted invitation in town, the event the music industry had been waiting for - the star studded, promotional showcase, extravaganza party for Big and his international smash CD5 *Love, Love, Lovin' You*. The party was also staged to pique interest in Big's first full-length album *A Little Bit of Lust and a Whole Lotta Love*, the exact release date to be determined when the record was finished and the furor over the CD5 subsided, which didn't seem likely for many months. Hundreds of rock stars, record executives, and music industry media people flocked to the doors of the Starshine Ballroom to witness the first ever live performance of the most popular artist on planet earth.

"Hellie, you still there?" asked Alex as she stood crushed in a crowd of people around the guest list table, her hair a mixture of apprehensive orange and stress magenta.

"Yes," peeped from somewhere below.

Alex turned and spotted Hellie behind her, sandwiched between two impatient record executives.

"I can't believe this, I don't wait in lines," said one of the executives as he pushed forward.

"Neither do I," said the other as he elbowed Hellie aside and nearly crushed her.

Alex felt the weight bearing down on her as she stood immobile in the crowd. "Hellie, this is crazy. Get against the back wall. I'll check us in and meet you there."

A muffled 'okay' came from behind someone's leather jacket.

Alex waited until the next impatient, self-important record company executive pushed by her. She stepped in his wake and was sucked through the crowd.

"Hi Chantille," said Alex as she popped out at the check-in desk.

An assistant Alex used to routinely pass in the halls during her days as a secretary greeted her warmly. "Alex, how are you?"

Alex gestured around her. "Good, but it's a little crazy in here."

Chantille rolled her eyes. "Crazy isn't the word, honey. It's a madhouse."

"How have you been?" asked Alex as she leaned back and tried to push off the weight of the people behind her.

"Still doin' the same old thing, but I'm good," she said as she thumbed through the guest list.

"Oh, I'm here with Hellie."

"Already checked her off. How's your new job?"

"Stressful," replied Alex. "I'm still getting used to it." She shrugged. "But I can't complain. It's what I wanted."

Chantille held out two plastic bead necklaces. As Alex reached for them, she felt a fist ram into her side.

"Ow," she said with a start. Alex looked behind her and saw a short, stubby, Napoleonic figure struggling through the sea of people crammed around her. His head burst forth under Alex's armpit, a hardened ball of snot dangling precariously from his right nostril.

"Marty Flanker," he barked in Chantille's direction.

Alex nearly lost her balance as Flanker pushed in front of her, his head coming no higher than her chest. Chantille silently handed him a necklace.

"VIP pass! Where is it?"

Chantille checked the guest list. "Sorry, sweetie, but you're not on the VIP list."

"WHAT?!" roared out of Flanker's mouth as a ball of snot shot out of his nose and over Chantille's head. "Of course I'm on the list. I'm ALWAYS on the list." Flanker leaned menacingly toward Chantille. "Get me a pass and get it now!"

Chantille leaned back in her chair and called over a supervisor. He thumbed through his stack of papers.

"Sorry, Mr. Flanker, you're not on the list. VIP area is senior vice president and up. You're a vice president."

Marty Flanker stood his full four feet eleven inches and clenched his fists. His face was quickly turning crimson.

Alex looked at Chantille and rolled her eyes. Marty Flanker, for all his money, perks, and position, had turned into a child and was nearly driven to tears because he couldn't get a VIP pass. Alex listened to him screaming and yelling, thankful he hadn't hired her as his assistant.

"Thanks, Chantille," said Alex, taking two plastic necklaces Chantille handed her.

"Show them at the door." Chantille flipped through some papers. "Oh, Alex, the girls never gave you anything for your promotion. Here, take these."

Alex almost burst out laughing when Chantille handed two laminate VIP passes over Flanker's head. She quickly put them in her blazer pocket.

"Hey, those are mine, give them to me!" screamed Flanker.

Alex gave Chantille a quick wave of thanks and threw herself against the crowd that was pressing in from behind her.

Flanker continued yelling. "Where do you think you're going with my passes?!"

Alex was quickly swallowed up as the mass of people lunged toward the table. She heard Flanker's muffled screaming grow fainter as she forced her way out of the mob. She popped out of the crowd and took a deep breath.

"Didn't think I was going to make it," said Alex as she caught her breath.

"I was getting a little worried," said Hellie as she walked toward Alex.

"I'm fine." Alex held out one of the necklaces. "We've got to put these on to get through the door."

Alex and Hellie wrapped the necklaces around their wrists and joined the people streaming into the room which once hosted orchestras and evenings of ballroom dancing but now held alternative and rock music shows. They raised their beaded hands as they passed through the wall of security guards blocking the doors.

Starshine had been transformed into a fairyland, with hundreds of yards of sheer white chiffon draped and weaved in and out, up and

152

down, across the expanse of the ceiling. Thousands of tiny white lights peeked out from the runners, stars twinkling in the heavens.

On the side stage was an orchestra, softly playing big band numbers as people entered and milled about the expansive room. The guests were appropriately dressed for the occasion in music industry black. Even the Yakadans had hung up their Elvis costumes and adorned themselves in black for the evening. Alex thought the color quite suited their green-tinged skin. It also looked like the aliens had dyed their hair black for the occasion, wearing it conservatively, yet stylishly, short, exactly like Big's. Even the women had Big hairdos.

"Alex."

Alex turned around. "Hey, Brett," she said with a short wave.

"Who's that?" asked Hellie as the very attractive Brett waved back and continued walking toward one of the many bars set up inside the ballroom.

Alex smiled and looked at Hellie. "Why? You want me to fix you up?"

"Hey, Alex," came from their left.

"Hi," said Alex as she gave another short wave to a group of four.

"No, I don't want you to fix me up," said Hellie blushing.

"How's it going, Alex?" came from their right as they walked further into the large room.

"Hiya," replied Alex in the general direction.

"So why not?" asked Alex.

"Why not what?"

"Get fixed up with Brett. He's single, just broke up with someone, even has a brain I hear."

Hellie laughed. "I'm not interested right now."

Alex raised her eyebrows. "Affair on the side?"

Hellie smiled and shook her head. "No. I don't have the time."

"Too busy saving the world?"

Hellie continued to smile. "No, just myself."

"Interesting," said Alex.

"What about you?" asked Hellie.

"What about me?"

"Why don't you go out with Brett?"

Alex's eyes wandered over the faces surrounding her. "Not interested."

Hellie gave her a smile. "Someone else, perhaps?"

Alex blushed. Several strands of purple appeared in her hair. "That's none of your business."

Hellie's smile widened. "You've got a crush on Skeater, don't you? It's written all over your face."

Alex's blush deepened. "I said it's none of your business." She leaned closer to Hellie. "Until something happens, of course."

Both women laughed and continued their tour of the room, their progress slowed down by the hundreds upon hundreds of people blocking their way. The crowd looked indistinguishable, with everyone in black and wearing the same expression of ennui and music business jadedness. Alex waved a half-hearted greeting to people right and left.

"How in the world do you know so many people?" asked Hellie as they weaved in and out.

Alex put down her mildly aching arm and looked at Hellie. "Some I know from hand delivering all those Langley memos."

"You know this many people from wandering the halls?"

Alex laughed when she saw the awe in Hellie's eyes. "More than you'd believe."

"What about the others?"

Alex shrugged her shoulders. "I guess once you get to manager everyone becomes your friend." She gestured toward the room. "I don't know half these people saying hello."

"But how…"

"I guess they recognize me from my picture in the promotion announcement database."

Hellie nodded. "You seem awfully popular."

"An illusion, I assure you." Alex leaned in a little closer. "Like most of this business."

The VIP section loomed ahead, powerful, commanding, the goal of any music industry executive. The elite were protected by a wall of security guards standing shoulder to shoulder against the gold railing that separated the almighty from the masses.

"Why is there a VIP section at a VIP party? Isn't everyone here considered very important?" asked Hellie as she and Alex looked at the impenetrable wall of muscular protection.

"Beats me," said Alex. "Maybe the V-V-VIPs don't want to be seen with the VIPs."

"It doesn't make sense."

"Does anything in this business make sense?" asked Alex.

"You've got a point."

"Anyway," said Alex as she pulled the laminates out of her pocket. "Seems we're V-V-VIPs tonight."

"How in the world?"

"Seems my fellow memo deliverers wanted to give me a present for getting promoted."

Hellie laughed. "How nice." She started toward one of the food tables set up around the room. "I'm hungry. Let's eat first."

"What should we have," asked Alex, conscious of the weight she'd put on working for Langley, but not able to pass up an opportunity to gorge good food for free.

She spotted a table full of salads and all things vegetarian. "Hey, I think they've got a veggie table," said Alex with surprise as she wandered across the room, her eyes searching for someone as Hellie followed at her heels.

*

Jiglio sauntered into the party, a leggy, dyed blonde hanging off each arm, a smug grin of satisfaction plastered on his face. The Senior Senior Executive President of Promotion headed immediately for the VIP area, ignoring everyone and everything until he was in the sanctuary of the elite. It had taken a few phone calls, several favors, and quite a bit of cash, but everything was in place for the evening's show. The show DiMachio hadn't planned.

*

Deity and Ruling Dictator DiMachio and Vice-Deity and Vice-Ruling Dictator Jeremy Wickett arrived at Starshine a Deity-acceptable one hour late. If they arrived too early, they might have to make idle conversation with other people, and if they arrived too late, they wouldn't have enough time to make an entrance, be noticed, and receive a little adulation from the masses. DiMachio knew the party was more for him than for Big, so he basked in the glory of his night as toast of the town. Celebrities come, celebrities go, but within the walls of the music industry, the power brokers were as important, if not more so, than the stars they created.

DiMachio and Jeremy Wickett waited several minutes, making sure their limousine caught the attention of the throng of photographers lined up four or five deep on either side of the red carpet that led into the venue. Five of DiMachio's steroid-laden bodyguards blocked the way to the main entrance, making the line of partygoers wait. Once the red carpet was clear of people, and DiMachio had run his fingers through his hair plugs, making sure the bald spots were covered, he was ready. He pressed his security beeper button, signaling his sixth bodyguard to open the door. He and Jeremy stepped out of the limo to a barrage of flashing white lights.

Hosannah appeared from nowhere and stood by DiMachio, her head down and away from the cameras as her boss always ordered.

"Update," said DiMachio softly enough so only his assistant could hear. He bowed his head next to Hosannah's shoulder and nodded gravely, as if she were telling him something vitally important. He made sure his profile was visible to the cameras.

"Place is packed, ready for your arrival."

"And Big?"

"On his way. You have half an hour before he gets here."

"Good," said Deity DiMachio. He and Jeremy Wickett nodded again, looking very, very serious and very, very important.

The crowd responded with a less than enthusiastic cheer, and the flashbulbs stopped flashing, but Deity DiMachio didn't notice. If a crowd gathered, and he walked by, they must be there to see him.

DiMachio stepped through the glass doors and saw Heysannah driving over toward him. When she pulled up alongside, he and Jeremy hopped in the back of the transmobile. DiMachio's bodyguard discreetly stepped on the back of the cart while Hosannah joined her twin sister in the front. They drove directly into the main room, making sure to merely nudge, not maim, anyone standing in the way.

DiMachio made an obligatory circle of the room, Jeremy, as always, nearby, and shook hands with the throngs of Acht employees, musical hangers-on and media hounds who all wanted a piece of the Deity. Cameras flashed in his face as they slowly drove around the room. DiMachio greeted them all, mumbling a few words of unintelligible idle chat, but never looking them in the eye.

As Deity and Ruling Dictator DiMachio rolled by the vegetarian food table, his trail of leeches and faithful followers directly behind, he heard a short, dry cough. He turned and saw a tall, gangly man, uncomfortable in his new tailored suit, having mango slices piled onto his plate by one of the many invisible waiters. Next to Clef stood a voluptuous blonde patiently waiting for the exotic fruit.

DiMachio banged his fist on the back of Heysannah's seat. "Heysannah. Turn left."

The transmobile turned and glided over to the food table.

"Clef," said DiMachio, extending his hand. "Glad you could make it on such short notice."

The ex-indie kingpin turned to face DiMachio, a twitch attacking his right eye. "DiMachio," said Clef as he grasped the Ruling Dictator's hand. "Wouldn't miss it for the world."

"Glad to hear it," said DiMachio.

"DiMachio," came from the Deity's other side.

DiMachio leaned over and shook the outstretched hand of his Senior Senior Executive President of Business Affairs and Law, and General Counsel.

"Langley," the said Deity as he pointed to his left. "I think you know Clef, owner of Black Dog Records."

"Sure," said Langley through two burning cigarettes. "Good to see you again."

The crowd surrounding the transmobile took a step back. Langley walked around the cart and shook hands with Clef.

DiMachio continued. "What you might not know, Langley, is that Clef is our new Senior Senior Executive President of A&R."

Langley looked at DiMachio with genuine surprise. "What about Skeater?"

DiMachio waved his hand dismissively. "Skeater's no longer with the company."

Langley masked his shock and again extended his hand to Clef, this time with much more enthusiasm. "Welcome aboard Clef. If there's anything you need, I'm here." Langley puffed harder on his cigarette and moved closer to the ex-Roadrunner of Rock, now A&R executive. He gave Clef a friendly pat on the back, initiating the corporate male bonding process. "Let's get a drink. I'll explain the ins and outs of being an Acht executive."

"Good idea," said DiMachio as he waved them toward the VIP area. "Go back where you belong and talk."

DiMachio glanced briefly at the food table. The voluptuous blonde, her hair streaked blue, magenta, and purple, stared at him open-mouthed, her full plate of food tilted and ready to fall onto the floor. He dismissed her from his view and his memory by turning his back and continuing with Jeremy on his obligatory rounds.

*

"Are you okay?" asked Hellie as she joined Alex, her plate full of pasta from the pasta table. She gently elbowed her coworker. "Alex, did you hear me?"

Alex snapped out of her daze and straightened her plate just as food began to slide off. "Huh? Oh, yeah, I'm fine." Alex turned back to the vegetarian table. She pointed to the tofu turkey. Silver tongs lifted silently in the air and piled more food onto her already full plate. She then pointed to the vegetable quiche and was given more by the ever attentive yet totally invisible waiter.

"Alex, what's the matter?"

"Nothing," said Alex. "Nothing I didn't expect."

"I don't get it," said Hellie. "You look like someone's died."

Alex smiled sadly. "Maybe someone has," she muttered to herself. She looked at her overflowing plate of food and then at Hellie. "Come on," said Alex with forced cheerfulness. "Nothing's going to ruin this evening. Let's devour this and attack the dessert table." Alex turned and hurried toward the nearest empty table.

*

At nine-thirty, exactly one and a half hours after the festivities began, Big's stretch limousine pulled up outside the ballroom. Timing was key to a superstar's impact, so the clonebot waited until the party organizers signaled he could enter. When he stepped out of the car with his date, the crowd raised its voice in a unified cheer of ecstasy. Police pushed on the blue barricades as people surged forward to try to get a better glimpse at their idol. Flashbulbs exploded all around.

Inside Starshine, a spotlight was turned on, its beam directed to the main entrance of the venue. The band struck up an orchestral version of Big's current number one hit, a song that had topped the *Billboard* charts for seven weeks and saw no signs of fading, "Love, Love, Lovin' You", the title song from his mega-mega million selling EP by the same name.

Alex and Hellie were positioned at a key table, next to the double wall of bodyguards creating an unobstructed path down the red carpet to the VIP section. When hearty applause and cheering broke out across the room, the two women stood on their chairs to catch a glimpse of the current Acht superstar.

The spotlight followed Big as he walked down the carpeted path. The crowd, who earlier had looked bored and jaded, turned into a mob of adoring fans who welcomed him with open arms and loving cheers. Hundreds of flashbulbs burst with momentary brightness as people called out Big's name, each trying to grab a little piece of his fame. Big waved royally to the guests, his well-practiced, full-white Hollywood smile lighting up his face. A hand holding a rose popped out between two security guards. Big's smile grew another inch as he gently clasped both hands around the fingers. He leaned over and sensuously kissed the back of the hand. Big straightened up with the flower as the hand went limp and fell to the floor, joining the woman who had fainted. He turned to his date and presented her with the rose.

Alex nearly fell off her chair. "Did you see who he's with, who he just gave that rose to?"

Hellie strained to see over the exceptionally tall security guards. "Oh, my, now that's a surprise," she said.

"Hi guys." Zena waved cheerfully as she passed by, clad in short, black, see-through lingerie. Big looked in their direction and also waved a hearty greeting.

Alex and Hellie nodded hello to Zena.

"How in the world did she finagle that one?" asked Alex, truly shocked.

"Jiglio, I'm sure."

They both watched as Zena and Big were escorted back to the VIP section, Bret Horowitz, entertainment lawyer, Harvey Gildsteen, manager, and Big's ever-growing entourage of businesspeople and leeches trailing right behind.

"What do you think she did?" said Alex as she stepped off her chair. She felt a wave of sadness wash over her. If only she had gone to his office right away, if only she had made more of an effort.

Hellie shrugged as she joined Alex back on the floor. "Maybe lingerie makes more of a statement than we realize."

Alex looked at her friend and shook off the melancholy that enveloped her. There was plenty of time to think about Skeater, and she was standing in the middle of the party of the year.

"You're probably right," said Alex, trying to force herself to have a good time. She pulled the laminates out of her pocket. "And it's not like we can't join her."

The two women clipped on their passes and made their way to the VIP area.

"Hey, you, those passes are mine."

Alex glanced behind and saw Marty Flanker rushing across the floor, a grease-stained linen napkin tucked under his chin and a turkey drumstick in his hand.

"Quick, let's go," said Alex as she rushed Hellie along.

The two women reached the impenetrable wall of six foot five, three-hundred-pound security guards and pointed to their laminates.

The guards briefly eyed them up and down, but one of them stepped aside slightly, giving them just enough room to get through.

"Stop, thief. Those are my laminates!"

Alex and Hellie rushed through. The wall of guards immediately reformed their security line.

"No pass, no entrance," was the last thing Alex heard as she and Hellie forced their way into the hundreds of people crammed into the small area.

"This is silly," said Hellie as they pushed their way toward the bar. "The whole party seems to be here."

"I know," said Alex as she ducked and weaved, trying not to get elbowed in the eye. "I thought it was crowded on the other side, but this is ridiculous. I can barely move."

The two women forced their way to the bar and stood behind a wall of elite partygoers ten people deep.

"This is what we've been missing all our lives?" said Alex as she looked around.

The private area was no more than a thousand square feet, and at least two hundred people - radio personalities, important journalists, music business executives, and stars - were crammed into the small area. Seventies folk singer Sam Brindell looked ruggedly handsome as he sat at a table, unshaven and unkempt, like he had just gotten off work from the car factory. He was deep in conversation with rock legend Dirk Preen, the 80s heavy metal spandex god who had broken up with his band in the early 90s to pursue metal lounge music, a genre Dirk had invented and the public had never quite caught on to.

Stadium rock guru Toro walked over to join the two superstars, his tight blue polyester shirt showing off his deteriorating muscles and expanding waistline. Toro had made a name for himself by revolutionizing rock and roll. He and his band, Hard, had brought old fashioned rock and roll back to the masses by being talented, writing great songs, and playing powerful music. But over the years Toro had become a caricature of himself until he was no more than the reflection of a shallow icon. His music changed with him, becoming only a shadow of what it once was.

A balding, middle-aged man with a face shaped like a leech, his mouth puckered and sucking, slithered toward their table but was stopped several feet away by a security guard. Without exchanging a word, the record company executive slunk away, his eyes searching the room, seeking out his next victim.

Alex looked at the faces seated at the dozen or so tables dotted around the far end of the VIP area and recognized 60s rock diva Gina Burn, still elegant and beautiful decades later. She was laughing with Toni Hirshel, the groundbreaking female icon whose songs made being a woman something to be proud of. Next to them sat the ever flamboyant and out of control drummer Oscar Pipe and the renowned singer songwriter Eddie Loove. On a closer look, Alex realized Oscar's hands were tied to his chair, and his chair was bolted into the floor. Drummers, they were all alike.

The only other personality Alex could easily spot was Winona Brisbane. She was hard to miss as she flitted amongst everyone, laughing, joking, and being the chatty talk show host that she was.

The last table, the one in prime position at the far end of the area, that had a view of the stage and all that was going on in both areas, with invisible waiters doting on the guests hand and foot, was three tables pushed together. It was a table fit only for Big and Deity DiMachio, the stars of the evening. Alex saw her former boss Langley, three cigarettes and a scotch in hand, talking to an uncomfortable Clef and giddy Weena. The Senior Senior Executive President of Media Relations, body parts intact and looking like an old, super-sized wannabe groupie, giggled like a teenager, her excitement at being seated with the elite of the elite obvious. Jiglio was next to Derby, as icy and dark as ever, a sinister glow emanating around him. DiMachio and Jeremy Wickett were at the end of the table, flanked by Zena and Big's ever-growing entourage of managers, agents, publicists and general executive hangers on.

Bored, Alex looked away and stared at the backs still blocking her way to the bar.

"We'll never get a drink," said Hellie.

"I know," said Alex. She turned around and groaned. "Oh God, he spotted me."

"Who?" asked Hellie.

Before Alex could answer, Derby pushed his way through the crowd and stood in front of Alex, blocking her way.

162

"Hi, Alex," he said, his fork trembling excitedly behind his ear. "Let me get you a drink."

"No, no, that's okay," said Alex as she tried to get by him. "I've got to meet some people out on the other side."

Derby took a step closer and put his hand on Alex's waist. "I insist." He leaned into her ear. "It's just a drink. Think of all I've done for you."

Alex cringed as she felt Derby's hand squeeze her flesh and begin to work its way around to the small of her back. "Really, Derby, I've got people waiting."

Derby gripped Alex tighter and pressed himself against her, rubbing himself up and down the front of her.

Alex felt like throwing up as she felt his hardened organ rubbing against her. She frantically searched for Hellie but couldn't find her as people continued to crush around them. "Derby, please, let go of me."

Derby smiled playfully and continued to rub himself against her. He again leaned into her ear. "No pressure; I've got plenty of time." He leaned back and looked into her eyes. "But you owe me, remember that."

"There you are," bellowed through the crowd as Weena knocked people right and left and forced her way to Derby's side.

Alex felt Derby let go and step back slightly.

"Weena, I've been looking all over for you," said Derby. "You look wonderful tonight."

Weena blushed like a schoolgirl and linked her arm through his. "Come on; DiMachio's at the table and he's asked where you were." She yanked him toward the executive table.

Just before Derby was sucked into the crowd, he turned to Alex. "See you later," he said greasily as he disappeared into the mass of people.

"What did Derby want?" asked Hellie as she pushed her way forward to Alex's side.

Alex stared at Derby as he disappeared into the crowd. "I have a feeling my promotion has some strings attached to it." She shivered with revulsion. "Let's get the hell out of here."

The two women weaved in and out of the throng until they reached the wall of security guards. As they exited the small space the guards made for them, Alex saw Marty Flanker, battered and bruised, throwing himself against the thighs of the guards.

"I belong back there! Let me back!" He bounced off the legs of the guard and landed on the floor, his legs sticking up in the air, his drumstick still grasped tightly in his hand. He ripped off his dirtied and torn napkin and stood up. He pawed the ground with his foot and again charged headfirst into the wall of guards. The guards took no notice.

"Flanker," said Alex as she watched him bounce off an overly muscular thigh and fall face first onto the floor. She unclipped her laminate pass and took the one Hellie was holding out. "Here."

Flanker looked up. "YOU!" he screamed as he charged forward.

Just as Flanker reached her, Alex stepped aside. He lunged past her and tripped over his feet, losing his balance. Alex heard the dull thud as Flanker fell onto his back, his arms and legs flailing about him. She saw the surprise in his eyes as he noticed his right hand still tightly clutched the turkey drumstick. With a small "Hmph" of satisfaction, Flanker brought the meat to his mouth and gnawed away at the flesh.

Alex walked up to him and held out the passes. "Here, take my passes, I don't want them."

Marty Flanker threw his meat aside and snatched the passes out of Alex's hand. He stood up, clipping both laminates to the lapels of his wrinkled and dirty blazer. He straightened and brushed himself off, the desperation gone from his eyes and replaced with cold-hearted executive anger. "They were my passes to begin with. If you so much as…"

"Whatever," said Alex as she turned her back and walked away.

"Why did you do that?" asked Hellie as she joined Alex and they walked back into the ballroom.

"You saw how pathetic he was."

"So why give him your passes?"

"Look."

They turned and watched Flanker, a woman now hanging off his arm, as he strutted through the security guards, his chest puffed out and his ego intact.

"He belongs back there with the rest of them," said Alex.

*

DiMachio and Jeremy Wickett were beside themselves, basking in the glow of power and fame as they held court and waited for Big to take the stage and perform four songs, two from his upcoming full-length album and two from his current smash CD-5.

When the venue lights went off, throwing Starshine into darkness, and an approving roar rose toward the ceiling, Deity DiMachio stood to get a better view and to be in better view of others. A spotlight cut through the darkness and aimed its beam at the well-dressed figure standing on stage, illuminating Big. The clonebot raised his hand and the taped music began, softly, slowly, heightened and augmented by the orchestra playing live on stage behind the superstar. Applause and wild cheering filled the room as Big began singing his number one smash hit, "Love, Love, Lovin' You" from his CD5 of the same name. The clonebot silently crooned and swayed as he almost sang the lyrics. Hardened women, whose faces were harsh and cold during the day, softened; some even swooned.

*

Alex and Hellie watched Big from their spot toward the front of the stage, but Alex couldn't concentrate on the show. She had been so stupid, thinking her promotion had happened because Derby thought she had a penis. It wasn't the penis he cared about; it was sex. Or it was both.

"What do you think?" said Hellie over the music.

"What?" said Alex.

"Alex, what's wrong?" asked Hellie.

"Nothing," replied Alex. "But I have to get out of here."

Alex turned and made her way out of the crowd, Hellie following silently behind.

The end of Big's song was lost to deafening cheers and applause as the crowd roared its appreciation. The next two songs were new tracks from Big's soon-to-be-released, first full-length album. He crooned his way through them, swaying a little offbeat but not moving

165

his feet. The orchestra welled up behind him, augmenting and enhancing Big's first-ever live performance.

DiMachio congratulated both himself and Jeremy as the audience soaked up the music. He realized that for all the problems there had been with Big's training, the Yakadans had achieved the near impossible; they had succeeded in making Big an international mega super balladeer rock star, though DiMachio knew most of the credit went to himself.

When the third song ended and DiMachio heard another deafening roar of approval, he knew the superstar created by his corporate music-making machine would bring him great green rewards, in large denominations. In the dark, he silently congratulated his best friend and true ally, Jeremy Wickett. Jeremy stiffened with gratitude and swung with approval as his master stroked their glories.

Big held up his hands to quiet the audience. They screamed even louder. He broke into one of his leading-man Hollywood grins. The screaming shook the rafters and vibrated throughout the entire room.

Big put his finger to his lips. The crowd settled. "I'd like to dedicate..."

The screaming began all over again.

Big waited until the audience had emptied their lungs, then continued. "I'd like to dedicate my fourth and final song..."

A chorus of groans and "No's" filled the air.

Big smiled his well-rehearsed sweet smile. "It's okay," he said, placating the audience with his deep, trained voice. "I'll be touring soon, once the album comes out, so we'll be seeing each other again."

Another round of cheering exploded from the crowd.

Big waited patiently, his hips angled and his shoulders thrown back, giving the audience his best pose. When the noise died down, he said, "I want to dedicate this song to my dear Zena, and to all the lovely ladies in this room."

Pandemonium broke out as women screamed, swooned, and tried to jump the stage. Security guards picked them up one by one and threw them through the air. Female bodies were hitting other women and splattering across the floor right and left.

Deity DiMachio watched the scene with growing excitement. Jeremy stood stiff at attention, ready to find some action. DiMachio looked to his left and saw Zena squirming playfully in her see-through lingerie. Jeremy was like a divining rod as he guided DiMachio down the table.

"He's wonderful, isn't he?" said DiMachio as Jeremy searched between Zena's legs for a warm, inviting home to enter.

Zena clapped her hands and turned toward DiMachio. "He's the best. I never knew he could sing so good."

DiMachio took Zena's head in his hands and gently turned it back to the stage. He leaned into her ear. "Why don't we watch the last song together?"

Zena nodded. She giggled as Deity DiMachio found her secret love spots.

Big belted out his fourth and final number, "Where There's Love There's Birds a Chirpin'," a middle of the road rocker with subtle yet strong electric guitar and heavy upbeat piano. DiMachio was fully aware of Big, his senses heightened as he engaged in his favorite decadent pleasure - casual sex with a stranger at a live show. He groped and fondled Zena as discreetly as possible, letting Jeremy run loose between her legs.

He kept his eyes on the stage and watched Big as the clonebot stomped and shook, waved and wailed, building up the crowd as he neared his crescendo. DiMachio and Jeremy were in perfect time, rocking and rolling to the sounds of their international mega super balladeer rock star.

The music soared to its peak, the violins and string instruments building up the collective tension in the room. The bass drum beat, the wind instruments wailed, the entire room was taken to unheard of heights of impassioned frenzy. DiMachio and Jeremy Wickett neared their peak, ready to explode their love juice. Big leaned back, his muscles straining, and hit his final note, his guttural enunciation of love. A blinding white light burst forth from the stage, forcing everyone to cover their eyes. Screams of pain rose through the air. DiMachio and Jeremy stumbled backwards and slid out of Zena.

"Gotta go," said Zena cheerfully as she patted the doubled-over DiMachio on the head. Somehow, the promotion assistant had managed to slip on a special pair of sunglasses during the final song. She skipped happily toward the backstage area, weaving in and out of people writhing in agony.

DiMachio blinked until his sight returned. He looked at the stage, two massive balls of black swirling before his eyes, and realized Big was gone. All that was left were the remaining bars of the last song and the smell of cooked meat.

His reptilian face hardened. He had memorized each second of Big's performance, especially the final few minutes. DiMachio and Jeremy had timed everything perfectly, but something had happened to Big, and he had a premonition it wasn't good.

The crowd had regained their composure and their eyesight and were cheering wildly for the international mega super balladeer rock star.

DiMachio and Jeremy Wickett rushed through the throngs of well-wishers, not bothering to acknowledge or accept their praise, and hurried backstage. As they made their way to the back of the venue, DiMachio caught a brief glimpse of Jiglio.

"Jiglio," DiMachio barked. "Where's Big?"

Jiglio looked casually at his boss and shrugged his shoulders. "Haven't a clue, it's a madhouse back here. I'm headed off to the after party."

DiMachio dismissed Jiglio by turning away. When he and Jeremy reached the backstage area, the place was in a state of utter confusion. People ran this way and that, yelling at the top of their lungs; Hosannah and Heysannah were holding each other and crying, and the orchestra musicians, blinded by the explosion, were bumping into each other and everything around them.

DiMachio spotted the Head Yakadan and interpreter TerraYak and made his way over to them. "What in the hell happened?" he yelled over all the confusion.

The TerraYak briefly glanced at the Head Yakadan and then faced the Deity. "Uh, Mr. DiMachio, we have a slight problem."

"How slight?"

"A little more than slight," the green-tinged alien answered in his typically monotone, unemotional voice. The Head Yakadan seemed to

168

give him a psychic push, so the TerraYak continued. "Big has disappeared."

"What do you mean, disappeared?" DiMachio barked. "Did he run away?"

"No, he disappeared permanently. That flash of white light at the end of the show, do you remember that?"

DiMachio nodded.

"That was the end of Big. It seems he disintegrated into thin air, a meltdown of such proportion that not a trace of him is left."

DiMachio felt the steam slip from his ears, but the more he thought, the more a smile fought to overtake his face.

"You mean to tell me," he said, needing clarification before he indulged in malicious glee. "Big is dead, gone, extinguished, never to be seen from again?"

The Head Yakadan and TerraYak nodded in silence.

DiMachio lowered his head, hiding the joy leaking onto his face. He felt like singing himself. He regained his composure and put on his corporate sympathy look. "I'm so sorry," he said as his mind raced over the potential lying hidden in Big's death. No more Gildsteen harassing him for money, at least not until he contracted out with another superstar, no more Milli Vanilli fake-singing records, no more hiding Big's inabilities.

It was a dream come true. DiMachio gave his condolences to the Yakadans and secretly left the building with Jeremy, nearly whooping for joy when he got into his limo. They rushed to DiMachio's penthouse apartment to have a celebration of their own.

*

Jiglio strolled out of Starshine at a leisurely pace, the sight of DiMachio frantically rushing backstage icing to his already sweetened cake. He hopped into the back of his waiting limousine. Only one part was left to his Master Plan. He picked up the car phone and dialed his own cell number.

When a voice answered, he said somewhat cryptically but in his usual icy tone, "Okay, one more to go. Do you have it?"

169

The female voice at the other end giggled brainlessly. "Of course I do, Jiggy. I remember everything you said."

"Good," replied the frozen, yet somewhat softening, voice. "Do exactly what I told you. When you're done, get in the limousine waiting for you and join me for a celebration at my place."

"What kind of celebration?"

"Do what you're told and you'll find out soon enough."

*

Zena clicked off Jiglio's phone and giggled to herself. If she slipped one envelope to the right person, without him knowing, she would be rewarded with an evening of unbridled passion with her lust-interest and boss. And she might get a Chanel outfit to go with her new Hermes bag.

She slipped her black lace lingerie strap off her shoulder and sauntered over to the backstage area, searching for the right person. No secret mission or covert errand was too much for Zena, though she didn't understand why Jiglio had her slip into Big's bedroom the night before and put odd computer-looking chips into his shoes and pockets of the blazer she knew he would be wearing at the Starshine party. When she tried to attach a small electrode-type gadget into the crease of Big's buttocks with super glue, he woke up. So, she seduced him, giving her evening an extra added treat, and allowing her first lady status at the party that evening.

Zena didn't care why she did what she did, dropping off envelopes to strange men in big, dark cars, fetching packages from seedy characters in alleyways and all the secret missions. It made her hornier than she'd ever been. And Zena's wardrobe grew with every assignment she accomplished.

She walked through the backstage area in her red stilettos, swinging the red Hermes handbag Jiglio had given her after their last rendezvous. Her silk and lace slip dress clung tight to her perfect figure as she searched the room for the intended target. When she looked over toward the corner, she spotted him, green-tinged with a triangular dark metallic-green pin fastened to the lapel of his blazer. She slunk over to the Head Yakadan and gave him a wave hello.

"Hi, Yakkie," she said.

The Head Yakadan turned and looked at Zena.

"Where's my hunk of a date, Big?"

The TerraYak rushed over to the Head Yakadan's side. "Miss Zena, I'm sorry, Mr. Big has left us."

"What do you mean, left us?" asked Zena, truly surprised. Jiglio said Big would be backstage, she was supposed to escort him to Jiglio's apartment where she had fantasies of getting two for the price of one.

The Head Yakadan put his arm around Zena as the TerraYak spoke. "I'm sorry, Miss Zena, but Mr. Big is no longer alive."

Tears of surprise filled Zena's eyes. "Oh, my, oh, my, I'm so sorry," she said.

The Head Yakadan held her tighter. Zena took advantage of the perfect opportunity and opened her pocketbook, taking out several tissues and a plain white envelope. As she noisily blew her nose, she placed the envelope in the inside blazer pocket of the Head Yakadan, carefully, discreetly, without the alien or anyone else seeing. She blew her nose one more time and dried her eyes.

"Well, guess I'll go home now," said Zena dry eyed and composed. She waved goodbye to the Yakadans and walked out of Starshine. When she hopped into the limousine and felt the cool leather underneath her hot, inviting thighs, she forgot about Big and her mission and concentrated on the wild, abandoned sex that lay hardened ahead of her between Jiglio's legs.

Eighteen

"As you're all aware, Big is dead."

DiMachio sat back and eyed his executives one by one, searching their faces for a hint of anything. They looked at him with nothing more than intense curiosity or executive boredom.

He leaned forward and clasped his hands on the conference room table. "It's a tragedy, a horrible, horrible tragedy." DiMachio let out a well-rehearsed and seldom used sigh of sympathy. "Big was so important to us, such a part of the family. We'll miss him."

The executives bowed their heads and nodded in agreement.

"He was like a brother to me," said Jiglio.

"I considered him one of my closest friends," added Langley.

"I don't know if I'll ever get over this," said Weena with tears in her eyes. "I feel like I might be responsible." She pulled a family size box of tissues out of her black canvas shoulder bag briefcase. "He loved me so much, I shouldn't have pushed him away. I left him alone in this cruel, cruel town." She pulled a tissue from the box and noisily blew her nose.

Derby reached over and patted Weena's hand. "There, there, it's not your fault. It's no one's fault. These things happen." Derby's fork sagged on his ear. "Big was my compadre, my drinking buddy, just one of the guys to me."

Clef raised his hand to his right eye, trying to cover the spastic twitching that had taken control of half his face. "Tragedy, horrible tragedy. Wish I had known him." The Senior Senior Executive President of A&R let out a short dry cough. "He would have been special to me."

The executives continued to repeat their fabricated stories so they could immortalize their connection with the superstar. DiMachio had become the father, Jiglio the brother, Weena the ex-lover, Langley the best friend, Derby the guy next door, and Clef the admirer who needed sympathy for being so close but missing out. In actuality, the executives had barely known Big, but once they convinced themselves their stories were true, their stories became true. Perceived reality was the only truth that mattered to them. DiMachio had made a career out of only believing what he wanted to believe, and he was pleased he had passed this ability on to his executives.

"Does anyone know what happened?" asked Clef.

DiMachio turned to Clef. "Meltdown," he said to his A&R executive. He looked at Clef's confused expression. "Langley will explain later."

Clef nodded.

"Do we know what happened?" asked Weena.

"Not yet," replied DiMachio. "What's important is what we do now."

"Do you want the post-mortem product development department involved?" asked Derby.

DiMachio looked at his Senior Senior Executive President of Sales and Marketing. "Why in the hell would I have a post-mortem product development department if I didn't use them?"

Derby looked blankly at DiMachio and said nothing.

"YES, I want them here! Who's in charge of it?"

"Sturgeon Westfield," said Derby.

"Then get him in here now!"

Derby was out of his chair and at one of the many guest phones placed around DiMachio's office. He spoke quickly into the receiver and was back in his seat in less than five seconds.

Within a minute, the door to DiMachio's office opened and an exuberant looking, yet respectfully sedate, Sturgeon Westfield walked slowly into the room, his panting the only evidence that he had sprinted up to the Deity's office. His black mourning suit and downcast eyes were perfect for the occasion.

Westfield stopped at the conference room table and looked at the Deity with exaggerated concern. "Mr. DiMachio and Mr. Wickett, let me offer my sincere condolences for your recent loss."

"That's Deity and Vice Deity to you," replied DiMachio.

"Yes, yes. Deity DiMachio and Vice Deity Wickett, may I offer..."

"Whatever," said DiMachio as he pointed across his round table. "Sit."

Westfield sat in the chair DiMachio pointed to, across the table and as far away from the senior executives as possible.

"Okay, Westin, give us our options."

"It's Westfield, Deity DiMachio."

"What kind of option is that?" DiMachio barked.

Westfield cleared his throat and shifted in his seat, his waterproof pancake makeup covered with beads of sweat. "We have several options. First, we should start with the funeral. It should be big, at St. Patrick's, with guest performers. We can make a tribute CD..."

"No funeral." DiMachio crossed his arms.

"But DiMachio," Derby started.

"I said no funeral."

Derby persisted. "But the money we can make from the record..."

"No."

"But..."

DiMachio glared at his Senior Senior Executive of Sales and Marketing. "Have you gone deaf?" DiMachio rose from his throne and leaned into Derby's face. "NO FUNERAL! You got that?!"

Derby nodded, his silver fork trembling.

Langley sucked furiously on two cigarettes. "Can you tell us why not?" he asked through swirling clouds of smoke.

"Not yet," replied DiMachio, glancing quickly in Westfield's direction. "We're telling the press he had a private service the day after his death. Big would have wanted it that way."

"Fine," said Westfield, looking a little less exuberant than he had when he first came through the door. "No funeral. What about memorial services?"

"What about them?" asked DiMachio.

"We could have public memorial services around the country, or the world, where people can come together and share in their grief. We could even sell tickets to it."

"I like that." DiMachio looked at his executives. "Derby, set it up. Make sure they sell tickets to get in and merchandise once they're in. Tell the public the money's going to some bogus charity. Weena, get press. Lots of it. And set up that charity. Make me chairman and head of the board of directors."

Both executives nodded and scribbled notes to themselves.

DiMachio looked back at Westfield. "What else?"

Westfield pulled out a perfectly ironed white handkerchief from his breast pocket and dabbed gently at his forehead, his perfectly manicured and expertly polished nails glistening under the fluorescent lights. "If you want to release another record but don't have anything recorded, we can tweak a few knobs and make sure you have material."

Deity DiMachio leaned back in his fur lined gilt trimmed leather throne and nearly laughed out loud. Jeremy Wickett swung back and forth in exalted glory. Big might have only one EP and one CD recorded, but DiMachio realized the potential was there for dozens more. It couldn't get any more perfect. DiMachio was so happy, he didn't even care who destroyed Big. It was turning out better than he could have ever hoped.

"That's enough, Westin," said DiMachio.

Sturgeon Westfield stopped talking mid-sentence and looked at the Deity.

DiMachio shooed Westfield away with a wave of his hand. "I said that's all. Go."

Westfield stood and left the room, his face downcast and depressed, his exuberance beaten out of him with five small words.

Deity DiMachio adjusted Jeremy and resettled on his throne, happy the intruder had finally left. Outsiders were definitely not welcome; they were only good for stealing ideas from.

"Back to business," DiMachio ordered.

His executives straightened to attention.

"*A Little Bit of Lust and a Whole Lotta Love*" needs to be released immediately." He glared at Derby. "No buts. It comes out in five days. I don't care if you have to go to the plant and help make the records; it comes out on Tuesday."

Derby nodded and jotted himself another note. When he finished, he put his pen in his mouth and began sucking furiously.

"I want them shipped to every square inch of this country. Second, radio needs copies by tomorrow, every radio station in the country, I don't care what the format. Tomorrow morning, I want the airwaves clogged with Big. I want obituaries and mentions in every newspaper in the world. I want Big's picture on every news show, in every magazine. I want the world plastered Big."

Langley stubbed out two Winstons at once. "How do we say he died?"

"We're not," said DiMachio. "I have a plan."

*

Alex was shocked to hear Big had mysteriously disappeared at Starshine the night before and was thought to be dead, but she had more important concerns to deal with. She had been pulled from her usual haggling with various departments over her assigned bands to help Big's product manager deal with the immediate release of Big's full-length record *A Little Bit of Lust and a Whole Lotta of Love*. Alex began running the halls of Acht at nine a.m. that morning, coordinating, disseminating, and liaising between every department, all the while making sure Derby was nowhere in sight. She returned to her office at six p.m. and found urgent phone messages stacked a foot high, while packages and memos cluttered up every free inch of space on her floor. She felt herself begin to tremble.

"Vernique!" said Alex as she stared at the mountain of papers and phone messages on her desk. "Damn it, get in here now!"

The perfectly attired, brain vacant assistant walked into Alex's office, her Coach shoulder bag in hand and Versace coat draped over her arm.

Alex spread her arms out over the pile of work stacked on her desk. "What in the hell is this?"

Vernique calmly inspected her perfectly polished violet nails that matched her perfectly violet contact lenses. "It's your work. What does it look like?"

Alex shook with uncontrollable anger. "My work? *My* work? What in the hell have you been doing all day?"

Vernique let out a bored sigh. "Taking phone messages and putting your mail in here. That's my job."

Alex leaned forward over her desk, her entire body trembling and consumed with rage, and glared at her assistant. "Did you ever think once, just *once*, that you could have helped some of these people instead of just taking messages?!"

Vernique looked at Alex coolly. "I did help. That's why I took the messages and put them on your desk." Vernique inspected her perfectly polished nails. "It's very simple. My job is to take messages; yours is to answer them."

Alex slammed her fist on the table, her voice hard and biting. "No! Your job is to support me, to help me get my job done!" Alex grabbed the messages and began thumbing through them. "Here's a request from a booking agent for CD's, a request from a vendor to check on an invoice, someone asking for our fax number!" Alex shook the messages in front of Vernique's face. "Couldn't you *at least* have given out the fax number?!"

Vernique rolled her eyes. "How should I know if you want me to give out the number? I wrote the message down, didn't I?"

The muscles in Alex's body went rigid. She felt a tightening in her chest as blood pounded in her ears.

"Get your damn coat off and get back to your desk."

Vernique rolled her eyes and stood calmly inside Alex's door. "It's six o'clock. I'm going home."

"The hell you are." Alex came around her desk and waved a stack of phone messages in Vernique's face. "You're going back to your desk and answering some of these calls."

Vernique stood her ground, a smug smile plastered on her face. "You can't force me."

Alex stood in front of her assistant, her body shaking. "No, but I can fire you."

Vernique let out a small laugh. "I doubt it. Don't you know who I am?"

"I don't give a fuck who you are, or who you think you are." Alex took a step forward and shoved the phone messages under her assistant's nose. "If I can't fire you, I'll make your life so miserable you'll wish I had."

Vernique stared at Alex, her perfectly painted lips pressed shut. Alex glared back, shaking with uncontrollable rage. With each second, she felt her blood pounding harder and harder through her veins. The ringing in her ears grew louder as the pressure built to an explosive level.

Vernique reached up and took the phone messages from Alex. "I'm out of here at six thirty." She turned on her heel and disappeared from Alex's office.

Alex sat at her desk and began reading the hundreds of emails that had been sent to her during the day. Her rage continued as she read email after email of unimportant, irrelevant, and repetitive gibberish. One or two phone calls to the right people would have taken care of at least 30 emails. She fumed as she picked up a pencil and snapped it in two. She closed her eyes as her stomach started churning. She felt herself getting angrier and angrier until she felt blood begin to pound in the veins in the side of her neck. She quickly opened her eyes and gasped with horror, remembering the last time she'd gotten so angry. She was turning into everything she had always hated.

She took slow, deep breaths. She cleared her mind and focused on pleasant thoughts. She continued her deep breathing until the pounding in her neck stopped and her stomach no longer churned. As she calmed down, she felt a presence inside her doorway.

"What?" said Alex, not looking up.

"Hi, Alex," floated across the room.

Alex groaned. "What do you want, Derby?"

"You."

Alex felt him move toward her. She looked up and saw his sweat covered silver fork trembling excitedly behind his ear as he sat on the edge of her desk.

Alex narrowed her eyes. "I'm warning you, leave me alone."

178

Derby leaned over and looked between Alex's legs. She noticed a flash of disappointment cross his face.

Alex stood up and leaned toward Derby. "What's your fucking problem? You're always staring between my legs, and it's starting to piss me off."

Derby's eyes were transfixed as he studied her groin area. "I just want to see it," he whispered.

"See what?" asked Alex in disgust.

Derby's face flushed red. "You know, your thing."

"What in the hell are you talking about?"

He continued in a hushed, reverent tone. "I know you have a penis. I saw the bulge that day. I just want to see it." He looked at Alex pleadingly. "Please. I won't hurt you. I won't even touch you. I just want to see it."

Alex stared at him.

"Just let me look at it," Derby begged.

Alex didn't know how things could get worse. She pointed to the door. "I haven't got one. Now get out."

"Yes, you do." Derby stood and moved toward Alex. "I saw it that day."

Alex stood, her feet planted firmly on the ground. "Stop, damn it."

Derby reached out and put his arm around Alex's waist, pressing his pelvis against hers, gyrating into her abdomen.

"Fuck you," roared out of Alex as she grabbed Derby and pushed him off her. With all her strength, she rammed her knee between his legs.

Derby groaned and doubled over. Alex grabbed his shirt and pulled him toward the door.

"It was my period, you asshole, not my penis. They were maxi pads."

Alex dragged him past Vernique and threw him into the hallway.

"Don't ever come near me again," said Alex as Derby crashed into the wall and crumpled into a heap on the floor.

"Cecil's on line one," said Vernique with uncharacteristic cheerfulness as Alex stormed by her and back into her office.

"What," she barked into the phone.

"Where in the hell have you been?" blew through the line and into Alex's ear. "All fucking day I've been calling, all day, and not one return phone call. What's wrong with you people there?"

Alex took a deep breath, but nothing could soften the acid coloring her words. "I've been busy today, Cecil. In case you haven't heard, Big died last night."

"I don't care *who* died last night," screamed the manager on the other end of the line. "I have an album coming out in a couple months, and the front panel looks like shit. Utter shit. Do you people know what you're doing!?"

"I'm doing my best." Alex stood rigid as she tried to control the rage bubbling up inside her.

"Well, maybe your best isn't good enough," blasted through the phone. "Maybe I need to put a call into Derby and DiMachio. Maybe then you'll stop being so lazy!"

The phone receiver trembled against Alex's ear. She had spent years being yelled at by a megalomaniac executive, had been corporately abused daily, had just been sexually assaulted, and was being screamed at by some lowlife, unimportant manager.

"Cecil," Alex barked into the phone. "Shut the hell up!"

"Who do you think you are, talking to me like that? You might as well kiss your job goodbye," screamed through the other end of the line.

Alex clutched the receiver, her heart pounding. "Hey, Cecil," she bellowed at the top of her voice. "Your band sucks!!!!"

Alex slammed down the receiver and let out a scream of frustration. She looked up to see Vernique applauding silently in the doorway, an amused look on her face.

"Guess we'll see who gets fired tomorrow, huh?" said Vernique condescendingly.

Alex had fire in her eyes. "You won't be around for anything tomorrow if I fire you tonight."

180

Vernique threw back her head and laughed, her hair perfectly in place. "You're pathetic. Just like everyone else here." She looked at Alex, brushing her away with a flick of her hand. "Don't bother with threats. I quit."

Alex stared at her assistant.

"Oh, yeah, one more thing," said Vernique. "You're the biggest asshole I've ever met." Vernique turned and disappeared.

"I'm the asshole?" Alex yelled toward her doorway. "You're the laziest piece of shit I've ever worked with."

Vernique's perfectly made-up face appeared briefly in Alex's doorway. "And you're the sorriest loser I've ever met. You might think you're so important with your job title and your office, but you're a big, fat nobody. And I mean fat." As the last words came out of her mouth, Vernique disappeared.

Alex rushed out of her office to an empty desk. She stepped over a whimpering Derby and ran toward the elevator. "Who do you think you are?" Alex yelled down the hall. "Little rich, silver spooned spoiled brat. You've had everything handed to you your whole life!"

Alex turned the corner as the elevator doors were closing.

"Loser," floated out from the car just as the doors shut.

"Fuck you," Alex yelled to the closed elevator. She stormed back to her office and slammed her door shut. She picked up her stapler and threw it across the room. In a blind fury, she grabbed anything she could reach and threw it across her office. Files, office equipment, trays, CDs went flying. As her trashcan bounced off the wall, Alex stopped abruptly and sat down. Realization flooded through her exhausted body. She wasn't just turning into Langley; she was turning into all of them.

Alex looked around her destroyed office. She picked up her backpack and put it on her desk. She rummaged through the pile of rubble strewn across the floor and pulled out some personal things and a handful of her favorite CDs. She stuffed everything into her bag and headed for the door. For the first time in a long time, Alex felt completely in control.

"I always blamed them," she said to herself as she looked around her office one last time. "But my only obstacle was me."

Alex opened her door. "And the only person who can do anything about it is me."

Something inside her cheered and seemed to do a backflip. Alex smiled. Even though she'd always known she was there, Alex finally found herself.

*

DiMachio clicked off his speaker phone and laughed out loud. Even he couldn't have schemed up a better way to make money. Big memorabilia were flying off store shelves as the world mourned the loss of the musician they now called a legend. And because the merchandising division of Acht had Big under contract, the company made money off each Big doll and Big paperweight sold.

Heysannah's entrance into the room interrupted the Deity and Jeremy Wickett's impromptu celebration.

"Thought you'd want to see this right away," said the Doublemint girl of rock as she placed the *New York Times* on his desk. She turned on her heel and disappeared back into the front office.

DiMachio looked at the front page of the newspaper and nearly whooped for joy. The lead story was a photo of Big and a headline screaming out in inch high letters BIG DEATH COVER UP. DiMachio flipped to the proper page and devoured the article.

"Reliable sources within Acht Records have expressed concern over the true nature of Big's death. Conflicting reports, coupled with the absence of a body, lead many people within the company to believe that Big's death was a carefully planned and executed plot to allow the singer anonymity from his overwhelming and unmanageable stress.

"According to sources, Big developed major phobias and fears that prevented him from being able to carry out his duties as the world's foremost superstar. The ailments escalated to a point where the singer became physically debilitated and was on the brink of a complete mental and emotional breakdown.

"In order to prevent the collapse of their leading superstar, Acht Records' Deity Vinny DiMachio agreed to stage the singer's death, thus giving Big the chance to start his life over again, this time out of the spotlight. When contacted for a statement, a representative for Deity DiMachio vehemently denied the accusations and gave a firm 'No comment' to repeated questioning..."

For the first time since he discovered Jeremy Wickett, DiMachio giggled with unabashed glee. He skimmed through the rest of the article until his eyes rested on a short sidebar piece. A blurry picture of a tall, muscular man wearing jeans and a windbreaker, his face concealed by a baseball cap and sunglasses, was shown eating caramel popcorn on a boardwalk. Directly below the photograph, in bold letters, was the caption, "Big in Delaware?"

The short article read, "A fan of superstar rock idol Big snapped this photo on the Rehoboth Beach boardwalk seconds after buying caramel popcorn next to this man at Dolle's Popcorn and Saltwater Taffy stand. 'I couldn't believe my eyes,' exclaimed Archie Marrs. 'There I was minding my own business, buying some popcorn, when this man stepped up next to me. I didn't think anything at first, but when I looked over at him and saw his size and saw how he held himself and how he spoke, I knew it was Big. I snapped the picture real quick before he knew what I was doing.'

When asked if he attempted to speak to the man, Archie replied, 'All that came out was the word 'Big'. As soon as I said it to him, he ran off, like I knew something he didn't want other people to know. That's when I was sure he was Big.' Representatives at Acht Records would not confirm Mr. Marrs' claims, though several other witnesses in the Delaware area claimed to have also encountered Big around the same time as Mr. Marrs."

DiMachio threw the newspaper in the air and exploded with a joyous "Yes!" as he congratulated himself on his genius. He had created the Big master plan. Rather than milking the memory of a dead man, Deity DiMachio had decided to plant a seed of doubt, following in the footsteps of Elvis Presley and Jim Morrison. If Big's death was questioned, exposed on some level as a cover-up, Bigmania would get bigger, and more records would be sold, more money would be made. Big's memory would be kept alive forever.

Deity DiMachio leaned back in his fur lined gilt trimmed leather throne and cackled with unabashed glee. He was going to be rich beyond his wildest dreams. And when future CDs came out, sung by the still-living hired singer, the seed of doubt would sprout and spread like wildfire. Everyone would buy Big's records to decide for themselves if Big had recorded the songs. And DiMachio would become even wealthier, maybe even the richest man in the world.

He hit his intercom.

"Yes, Deity DiMachio."

"Get that Westin on the phone, that post-mortem person."

"Putting you through, Deity DiMachio."

"Sturgeon Westfield," came somewhat shakily through the phone line.

DiMachio leaned toward his speaker phone. "Westin, it's DiMachio."

"Deity DiMachio, what a pleasure..."

"I'm sure it is," said DiMachio with his usual lack of patience. "I'm calling about Big."

"Is something wrong?"

"No, no," said DiMachio, chuckling. "Actually, just the opposite. Couldn't be better."

"Can I help you with anything?"

"Yes, you can." DiMachio smiled to himself, knowing this would be risky. "I want a list of musicians at Acht who are prone to accidents, who get sick a lot. You know, we don't want this Big thing happening to anyone else."

"Of course, of course, Deity DiMachio. I'll get to work on it right away."

DiMachio hung up and smiled. What's a death here and there if millions and millions of dollars are involved?

Deity DiMachio leaned forward and turned on his eight-screen television/surveillance system. All the networks had picked up the story; CNN was airing special live up-to-the-minute coverage on the Big phenomenon. Thousands of people had already flocked to the small resort town of Rehoboth Beach, Delaware, searching frantically for their lost idol Big.

DiMachio ordered an executive staff meeting. When everyone had gathered around his private office conference table, he unfolded the next phase of his Big post-mortem marketing plan.

184

"I'm sure you know Big's been spotted in Delaware. Since then, thousands of people have flooded the town. We need to capitalize on the collective buying power of all these people."

"What do you mean?" asked Jiglio, even his stone-cold interest piqued at the potential.

"Every town with a Big sighting must have plenty of Big memorabilia to sell, both records and merchandise." DiMachio shuffled through the mountain of Big press on his desk. "Fans are holding candlelight services in cities around the world, trying to 'make sense of a senseless death' as one paper put it. Another paper reported that fans are gathering to decide if Big is alive or dead. Thousands of people are getting together because of Big, and we need to capitalize on their collective buying power."

"Do you have anything in mind?" asked Weena.

"Derby, tell the merchandising division to start making Big memorial candles, to be shipped and sold everywhere." The Deity leaned back in his throne, another ingenious plot hatching in his greedy head. "I want Acht to start a travel agency, specializing in Big promotional tours. We'll arrange fan packages to whatever city Big is spotted in, taking a hefty commission off all travel arrangements and plans." The Deity leaned forward with a sarcastic smile. "Naturally, this is being done for Big's mourning fans. We're doing this as a service to his fan base, not to make money." DiMachio pointed at Weena. "Make sure press around the world knows how much we care about the fans. Make them think we're as concerned over Big as they are."

All heads nodded.

DiMachio pointed to the door. "Go."

Nineteen

Jiglio was the first to be called. When he walked into the executive boardroom, he was confronted with a row of straight lipped, gravely serious Yakadans seated next to each other on one side of the conference room table. There was a palpable feeling of tension in the air, a heavy thickness that clung to Jiglio as he moved toward the Yakadans.

For the first time he noticed how identical they were. They could have been clones, with their matching brown hair, squarish green heads, and general medium build. Even their heads were all tilted slightly to the left. When a TerraYak had phoned Jiglio's office less than ten minutes earlier, summoning him to the boardroom, the Senior Senior Executive President of Promotion had not been surprised. He knew the Yakadans had to gather evidence to fire DiMachio and hold him responsible for Big's annihilation, as Jiglio had implicated in his anonymous letter.

Jiglio stepped up and faced the row of aliens. He noticed a glass and a small carafe of water strategically placed in front of the only chair on his side of the table, so he took his cue and sat down, facing the owners of the record company called Acht.

The TerraYak directly across from him spoke first, verbalizing the sonar thoughts of all his colleagues.

"First, Mr. Jiglio, these proceedings are informal; we called you here for a friendly discussion."

Jiglio nodded, aware that they were all scrutinizing him. And for his plan to work, Jiglio knew he had to put on the performance of his life. His months of hard work trying to oust DiMachio could come down to this one interview. The Senior Senior Executive President of Promotion adopted his icy poker face.

The TerraYak shuffled through several papers. "First, we'd like to hear your account of what happened to Big the night he melted down."

Jiglio blinked and shrugged nonchalantly. "There's not much to say. The party was a party, like all parties." Jiglio smiled a rare, greasy smile. "Except, of course, it was bigger and better than anything I'd ever been to."

"You saw nothing unusual?"

"No." Jiglio blinked, then rubbed his right eye. "But I didn't actually see the meltdown. I had already gone backstage to congratulate Big on his performance."

"You did not watch until the end of the show?"

Jiglio looked at the expressionless aliens, amazed at their lack of knowledge about music. He figured they were the kind of people who would go to a show and actually sit through the opening act. "No. I never watch a whole show. Things get too crowded backstage so I get to the dressing room early, pay my respects as soon as I can, pose for photos, then leave. If I want time with an artist, I'll have dinner with them after."

"And that is what happened?"

Jiglio blinked. "I went to the dressing room, Big didn't show up, it got really crowded, so I left. I figured Big had gone somewhere with DiMachio to celebrate."

"You did not have dinner plans with Big?"

Jiglio shook his head. "No. We were waiting to see how Big felt after the show, how many people wanted to speak to him, that kind of thing."

"You didn't see anyone suspicious lurking around, someone who might not fit in with the crowd backstage?"

Jiglio leaned forward and poured himself a glass of water. He sat back and looked at the aliens. "No. Is there some kind of problem?"

The TerraYak paused briefly and glanced to the end of the table where the Head Yakadan sat staring at Jiglio. He looked at the Head Yakadan for a second, then returned his gaze to the promotion man in question.

"It's not that there's a problem; we want to be thorough in our report back to the Autobureat on our planet Yaka."

Jiglio knew he had to be careful, very, very careful. If the Yakadans suspected anything out of the ordinary with him, he might end up being charged with Big's death. "No, there's nothing unusual, unless DiMachio laughing and smiling and being in a good mood is unusual."

The Yakadans looked at each other solemnly.

Jiglio leaned forward and placed his hands on the table, his expression serious. "I was only joking."

"Was Mr. DiMachio in a better mood than normal?" asked the TerraYak.

Jiglio paused, as if thinking, then replied, "Come to think of it, he was in a really good mood, more so than usual." He dramatically brushed away his comment with a wave of his hand. "But it was Big's big night. Of course he'd be in a good mood. I mean, I'd say he was downright ecstatic that night."

"I see," said the TerraYak.

Jiglio knew he'd done as much as he could. "I don't understand the investigation. I thought Big had some technical malfunction."

The TerraYak looked directly into Jiglio's ice black eyes. "Perhaps. We must look at all angles. It's procedure. And with no parts of Big left for us to study, our task is much more difficult."

Jiglio blinked and took a sip of water.

"Well, Mr. Jiglio," said the TerraYak. "There's no point in us keeping you from your work. Thank you for your help and cooperation."

"If there's anything I can do," said Jiglio as he pushed back his chair and stood up. "Call me any time." The Senior Senior Executive President of Promotion nodded to each of the Yakadans behind the table and exited the room, a one-inch-wide festering boil simmering on his forehead.

After the promotion man left, the Yakadans picked up their pens and made identical notations on the pads of paper in front of them.

"Excessive blinking. Possible termination."

And so it went for all the executives: Langley chain smoking; Weena losing body parts; Derby sweating profusely; Clef developing contorting body twitches thought impossible to achieve by even a seasoned yogi. As soon as each left the room, the Yakadans made identical notations on their subconscious stress indicators, writing the words 'possible termination' next to each name. The aliens knew if they
188

didn't find the exact cause of Big's extinction all the senior executives would be fired, regardless of how long or short they'd worked for the company.

DiMachio and Jeremy Wickett had no choice but to be interrogated together; they were too close to be separated. When the call came for DiMachio to report to the executive boardroom with his right-hand man, he knew the situation was serious. Before he left his office, he made a couple of quick phone calls and discreetly put his emergency evacuation plan into operation, just in case. As the Deity and Ruling Dictator left his office, his two seldom seen, never heard bodyguard hulks entered his office and began destroying what needed to be destroyed and removing what needed to be removed.

Jeremy cowered limply at the side of his master as they took their private executive elevator up one floor to the executive conference room. DiMachio knew he would have to compensate for his confidante and friend's shrinking size and fading glory.

When the Deity stepped into the boardroom and smelled the awkward tension hanging in the air, he prepared himself for the worst. He sat in the chair vacated by Jiglio and the other executives only a couple hours earlier and faced the firing line of Yakadans.

Once again, the TerraYak spoke the thoughts on his side of the table. "Mr. DiMachio and Mr. Wickett, thank you for coming."

DiMachio said nothing while Jeremy Wickett was unable to say anything.

The TerraYak continued. "The Yakadan Board here on Earth and the Autobureat, our ruling government on Yaka, have discussed the untimely and most unfortunate demise of Mr. Big. We doubt we will ever know what happened to our clonebot, and we will most likely not be able to prove our suspicions, but we want you to know the seriousness of what has transpired.

"For many of your earth years, we have researched and studied the possibilities of creating clonebots to be used for the good of our planet. Thousands of our people invested their lives, and several lost theirs, to help meet this goal. In an attempt to thank the planet for allowing us to come here and make a second home for some of our citizens, we had planned to share our technology with your government once we had perfected it. But now that is gone. Y1K, or Big as you named him, took five earth years to make and was our only prototype.

Because our Autobureat is so displeased with the results of our experiment, and because so much time, effort and money were invested in it, we're not sure if we'll get another chance to do what we were trying to do here."

The TerraYak and Yakadans stared intently at DiMachio. "Do you understand what I'm saying?"

The Deity shrugged, bored with the attempted pity routine. "Yeah, I do. But what's that have to do with me?"

"Nothing, Mr. DiMachio, nothing," said the TerraYak, shaking his head. "What we'd like to know is what you saw happen the night Mr. Big melted down."

"Well," said DiMachio, relaxing a little. Maybe this was only a reprimand. "It was the final note of the final song in Big's performance. He hit a high note, and there was this huge, blinding flash of white light. I had to cover my eyes so I didn't see anything else. And then Big was gone." DiMachio found himself stifling a smile of joy of Big's demise into oblivion.

"And what have you gained from this, Mr. DiMachio?

"Excuse me?" said the Deity to the TerraYak.

"I said, what have you gained from Mr. Big's death?"

DiMachio knew exactly what they were insinuating and thought fast to find an appropriate answer, one that would mask his unquestionably joyful feelings.

"Well," said the Deity. "I've gained a sense of community and love from all the phone calls I've received, as well as all the flowers and telegrams. People were moved by the death of Big and bonded together through their love for the superstar to work through the pain of losing someone so important in their lives."

DiMachio felt a lump grow in his throat as he became caught up in the emotion of his own lies.

The row of Yakadans remained straight lipped and emotionless as they continued staring at every nuance in the Deity's face. "That's beautiful, Mr. DiMachio. What about materialistically? In that regard, what have you gained from Big's death?"

"Me personally?" said DiMachio, a look of mock surprise masking his face as he tried to think of something acceptable to say. He

190

looked at the unchanging, identical Yakadans, his expression changing to one of fatherly love and concern.

"The thought of material gain never crossed my mind. Now that I think about it, of course we'll make some money off increased record sales, but that can't in any way come close to the loss of such a major superstar and experiment." DiMachio looked at the aliens with hurt. "I would never think to make a profit off Big."

"Is it true you were named beneficiary in the event Big died, meaning you will receive all future record royalties from the singer?"

The Deity had forgotten about the day, only a month after Big was hatched, that he and the then upcoming superstar had decided to name DiMachio as the executor of his estate and sole recipient of all artist royalties should something unforeseen happen to the international mega super balladeer rock star. He wondered how the Yakadans found out about his pact with Big when Big's lawyer and manager hadn't, never guessing one of his senior executives had discovered the truth and used it to frame him.

"Mr. DiMachio, I repeat, is it not true you are the beneficiary of all future Big royalties?"

"Uh, I forgot about that," said the Deity, feeling Jeremy shrink smaller than he ever had before.

The Head Yakadan flipped through the file of papers in front of him. When he paused, the TerraYak continued speaking for him. "And is it also true that Mr. Wickett has been named the beneficiary on a two-million-dollar life insurance policy?"

DiMachio stared at the Yakadans, professionally controlling the anger that was beginning to well up inside of him. "An insurance policy?" he said with as much feigned surprise as he could muster. "I don't know anything about that."

The Head Yakadan slid the policy agreement across the table toward DiMachio. The Deity picked up the paper and glanced at it as if it were the first time he'd seen it.

"Well," he said as he studied the insurance policy. "It definitely has Jeremy Wickett named as beneficiary. But that's Wickett, not me."

"You two are one and the same to us Yakadans."

DiMachio knew the truth in the words they spoke and was unable to finagle his way around it.

"And is it also true that you will receive a three percent producer royalty from both his CD-5 and his album?"

The Deity shrugged, bored with the long-winded interrogation. "I guess so."

"Are not quarterly bonuses given out by you at your company to both yourself and your senior level executives, based on level of record sales and profits in that particular quarter?"

"Now wait a minute," said DiMachio. "You're making this sound worse than it is. All record companies have bonuses. And I worked hard with Big; executives can get a point or two for producing a musician's record. I helped with his voice lessons, his dancing, his stage presence; I was there for Big all the way. And I totally forgot about the beneficiary papers."

"Answer the question 'yes' or 'no'. Do you receive bonuses on a quarterly basis, in addition to your more than generous salary, a salary which you and your senior executives increased by twenty-five percent less than a year ago?"

"Yes."

The Head Yakadan passed a folder to the TerraYak. When the half alien, half earthling received the file of information, he turned back to the Deity. "We have a few questions about your expense reports."

There was no way out. Jeremy had shriveled so small he was barely visible.

The TerraYak shuffled through the papers. "In August 1991, did you expense off a trip for ten thousand dollars to Europe, a trip in which your secretary at the time accompanied you on, and one in which you never left the Chateau de Fromege in Switzerland?"

"How can I remember that far back?" asked DiMachio as his stomach acid began to churn, leaving a sour, metallic taste in his mouth.

"We checked with the business associates you supposedly had meals with over the last couple of years, and most of them were fabricated." The TerraYak flipped to the next piece of paper. "On Christmas Eve in 1994, you claimed to have taken your executive staff out for a Christmas meal, a meal which cost over a thousand dollars."

"I don't remember," said DiMachio.

"We checked with your staff. No one was at that meal. In March of 1995 you had a quote, unquote, business trip for five thousand dollars. We checked your records and the people you claimed to have meetings with. All lies. In the last two years we audited every one of your expenses items and found in two years alone you had over one hundred thousand dollars in unwarranted and fabricated expenses." The TerraYak looked up from his paper. "Do you understand what that means?"

"It means that someone that works for you has done their job wrong, or someone in this company is trying to frame me," said DiMachio.

"Mr. DiMachio, we have all the proof we need. We cross referenced your meals with the Acht people you claimed to have eaten with, and we found the vast majority of them had expensed their own meals that evening with people other than you."

The game was over, and DiMachio knew it. "What do you want?" he hissed with reptilian venom, his eyes narrowing with an evil few men could muster.

"Your resignation. We would prefer to give you the option to resign, rather than fire you and take you to court for embezzlement."

DiMachio seethed. "How can you do this to me? I had nothing to do with what happened to Big."

The TerraYak answered matter-of-factly. "If we had any proof you arranged Big's meltdown, we would take you to Yaka and have you killed. But we do not have enough evidence, and we do not want to ruin relations with your planet."

"So let me go on doing what I do best."

"No, Mr. DiMachio. You were responsible for our clonebot, and you failed in your duties. Therefore, you must be terminated from this company."

DiMachio glared evilly at the aliens. "And what if I refuse to resign?"

"You go to jail, as simple as that."

DiMachio began his Acht slow boil, steam escaping his ears. "What do I get in return?" DiMachio knew if the Yakadans were asking for his resignation, they would give him something in return. Almost all executives were spared the humiliation of being fired and the degradation of going to jail. The publicity could put the company in an unfavorable light. And the ruling minority always took care of their own.

The TerraYak looked at him matter of factly. "We are offering you ten million dollars, but you must sign an agreement stating you will never disclose any information whatsoever about Big, you cannot work in any position in the music industry for five years, and you will never discuss the terms of this deal."

"Ten million, that's all?" said DiMachio. "That's what I make in a year. You can do better than that."

"Terms are nonnegotiable, Mr. DiMachio," said the TerraYak. "It's very simple. You sign the termination and resignation agreement and receive your ten million dollars, or you go to jail." The TerraYak held out a pen to DiMachio. "The choice is yours, and you must make it now."

Venom dripped down the side of the almost-exDeity's mouth, his boiling anger replaced with venomous hate. He glared with unfathomable loathing at each of the Yakadans. He grabbed the pen from the TerraYak and angrily signed the agreement for himself and Jeremy Wickett. When he finished signing in triplicate, he slid both the papers and the pen back at the TerraYak.

"You will not return to your office, nor will you ever set foot in this building again," said the TerraYak as six bulky steroid laden Yakadan military guards came into the room. DiMachio and Jeremy Wickett rose and walked toward the door where the guards waited.

"Mr. DiMachio," called out the TerraYak.

The exDeity turned, his face so contorted and twisted with rage he was unrecognizable.

"Consider yourself lucky, Mr. DiMachio. There are places in the universe where excessive greed is punishable only by death. You're the lucky one. Your greed has made you a very wealthy man, one who never has to work again. And you can live to enjoy it."

DiMachio turned without responding. To a rich music man, money without power was useless. The former head of Acht Records stepped onto the elevator with his faithful friend, Jeremy Wickett. He leaned out the car door and spit on the floor, cursing the walls and everything within them. "I'll be back," he hissed aloud. "And we'll see who's sorry then."

The elevator doors closed and took the two unemployed, but very wealthy, music industry moguls down to meet their uncharted, unknown fate.

*

Jiglio waited in the lobby like an excited child. He'd been tipped off that DiMachio and Jeremy Wickett had gone to meet with the Yakadans, so he'd hid himself behind a pillar in the building lobby, just in case DiMachio met his end.

Jiglio nearly whooped for joy when he spotted DiMachio rounding the corner. All Jiglio's years of being in the shadows, of being under DiMachio's fist, were finally paying off. It was Jiglio's turn to rule; convincing the Yakadans to make him Deity would be easy.

As the heavily armed military guards rounded the corner behind DiMachio, first two, then four, then six, a sick feeling washed over Jiglio. If the Yakadans were taking DiMachio's dismissal that seriously, what if there were more repercussions? He spun around in shock, realizing what he might have done.

*

Skeater made his way down Cornville Road, a smile playing at the sides of his mouth, the warm sun tickling his skin. He said good morning to each person he passed and unfailingly received a friendly reply. The ex-Acht A&R man was still a newcomer in town, his arrival in Cornville, Arizona, still counted in weeks rather than months or years. But he noticed with each passing day that the townspeople were warming up to him and his strange city ways, and as each day passed, Skeater became more and more relaxed, more and more like the good-hearted people he was surrounded by.

Skeater wasn't sure how he and Skat landed in the small town of Cornville; he would never know exactly what happened on his dazed journey away from the corporate dungeon of Acht to the wide-open space, and peace and tranquility, of the desert in Arizona. He remembered the stacks of memos and papers engulfing him in his office, burying him alive under their weight, and he remembered his frantic escape with Skat from the confines and constraints of a conglomerate life. He had packed his old, beat-up duffel bag from his traveling days in the early eighties and rushed to Penn Station to grab the first train going west.

He went as far as Chicago and bought himself a used car, speeding out of the city, wanting to get away from so much man-made concrete and bad vibes. When he approached Kansas City, he threw road signs to the wind and explored secondary roads that led him through the Rockies. Once out of Colorado, he decided to stop for a few days in the first town he came across that suited his fancy. He couldn't remember what he saw in Cornville, but he loved the red rock area and decided to stay for a couple of months, until he felt like moving on.

As Skeater walked toward Windmill Park, he heard drums and chanting floating through the air. With Native American tribes like the Hopi and Navajo not too far away, Skeater knew the area was rich in Native American history and culture, but he had never heard music so mesmerizing and spiritual. He followed the sound to the Windmill Park parking lot and found a group of men playing music. Skeater stood transfixed as they played and chanted prayers to the heavens.

When they finished their song, the leader of the group turned and waved Skeater over. Skeater hesitatingly walked across the parking lot toward the men.

"Do you like our music?" asked the leader as Skeater approached and shook his hand.

"I don't know anything about it," said Skeater honestly. "But you sound amazing."

"Thanks," said the members of the group.

"Do you do this for a living?" asked Skeater as his body began to tingle.

The leader laughed. "No, no. We could never make money to live off this."

Thoughts churned in Skeater's head. "Have you ever thought of putting out a record?"

One of the younger group members laughed. "Who would buy this stuff? This is traditional Native American music, passed down for generations."

"Well," said Skeater. "I used to work at a record company in New York. If you wanted to make a record, we could do something together. I could start a small record company, promote and market you..."

As Skeater continued talking, he found himself growing more and more excited. He had money saved from years of making a needlessly exorbitant salary. And this time he would do it on his own, his way, the way it should be done. This time he was going to make much more than just money.

*

Alex threw her head back and laughed, her now probable blonde hair streaming behind her as she cruised through the last mile of southern Wyoming on her recently purchased and only slightly used Harley Davidson. As she sped south, toward parts and places unknown, Alex headed toward Denver to see if she wanted to stay a while and earn some money.

When she arrived, she felt calmer than in New York, but she could still feel the materialism and competitiveness any city must have to survive. She stopped at a gas station to fill her tank and stock up on water and necessary supplies. Alex walked into the station mini-mart and picked up a few bottles of spring water and a carton of yogurt.

As she walked down an aisle, she caught her reflection in the glass of the refrigerator section and smiled. If she didn't buy a pair of jeans soon, she would have to tie her old pair on to her body. Alex hadn't been conscious of losing the weight, but the pounds had melted off as she headed further and further away from the stress and cause of her unhappiness. She walked to the front with the magnetic air of someone confident in herself and content with her life.

"How you doing today?" asked a kindly senior citizen behind the cash register.

Alex put down her items and smiled warmly. "Never felt better."

"That's good to hear," smiled back the gentleman cashier as he rang up her purchases.

"Oh, I forgot," she said to the cashier. "I want to get a newspaper."

The cashier waited patiently as Alex walked over to the newspaper section. As she picked up a Denver paper, she saw a lone

Billboard magazine among the other papers and magazines. She reflexively reached for the weekly music industry trade magazine that she had faithfully read for years. The front-page headline that screamed out at Alex shocked her.

Her heart pounding, she picked up the magazine and added it to her purchases. When Alex got outside, she moved her bike to the side of the lot and sat down on a small patch of grass, the sun wrapping its rays around her and keeping her company. She pulled the magazine out of her bag and read the headline once again. "Shake Up at Acht Records".

She dove into the article, savoring each word in front of her. "Last Monday five of the top executives at Acht Records were dismissed. The official announcement came late that afternoon when a spokesman for the record company issued a statement saying, 'Due to a company-wide reorganization, Sal Langley, Senior Senior Executive President of Business Affairs and Law, and General Counsel; Ilsa Weena, Senior Senior Executive President of Media Relations; Horatio Derby, Senior Senior Executive President of Sales and Marketing; Bennie Jiglio, Senior Senior Executive President of Promotion; and Clef, Senior Senior Executive President of A&R, mutually agreed to terminate their contracts with Acht Records. No decision has been made as to their replacements.'

As we reported in last week's *Billboard*, the Deity and Ruling Dictator of the company, Vinny DiMachio, and the Executive Vice Deity and Executive Vice Ruling Dictator, Jeremy Wickett, also agreed to part ways with the company. Mr. DiMachio has since been replaced by Frances Guyere, the former president of the accounting firm Bernstein Bernstein & Bernstein. He has been given the title President and CEO of Acht Records..."

Alex looked at the photos of the six executives, for security reasons Jeremy Wickett was never photographed, and studied the faces she had dealt with for almost two years, the faces that had caused her so much frustration and pain. They were strangers to her, distant memories that meant nothing. Their future was their own, and the ex-assistant to Langley realized she felt nothing toward any of them, no sorrow, no anger, no emotion at all.

Alex skimmed through the rest of the article, shocked at the news but knowing their severance packages would be in the millions. As she turned the page, another article caught her eye. "Acht Executives to

Turn Around Blurb Records." Alex wasn't surprised to read that all the former Acht executives had been immediately hired at Blurb Records.

And they wonder why the music industry is so bad, Alex thought as she read about their new jobs at the major label. The industry recycles the same incompetence over and over again. It wasn't about the music to those people; it was about money and power. And it's the bands and fans that suffer.

As Alex flipped to the end of the magazine to read the rest of the article, she stumbled across a photo of her Acht friend Hellie with her tank full of mutant sea creatures. The accompanying article was about a new form of alternative music where dance, art, music, and sideshow were blurring together to form a new trend called dams.

Alex read through the piece with a smile on her face. After many months training her mutant sea creatures, Hellie had been put under contract by the Danceartrock organization and was preparing to go on tour with that year's lineup as the star of the second stage.

The highlight of her show was reported to be the sea creatures' choreographed version of "Bohemian Rhapsody". Hellie had left her job shortly after Alex. According to the magazine, Hellie wanted to concentrate full time on her dancing mutant sea creatures. The demand for her creatures at parties, fairs, and cultural events was already so high Hellie was scouring the Hudson for more creatures to train.

"Congratulations!" Alex called up to the sky, hoping the wind would blow her love and salutations across the space that divided them.

Alex ripped out the article on Hellie and tucked it into the pocket of her jeans. She walked back to the front door of the mini-mart. She stood several feet away, took aim, and scored two points as the magazine that had been so important to her for so many years landed squarely in the trash can that stood by the glass doors.

Alex walked over to her bike and safely stashed her packages in her storage compartment. As she put the Denver paper in, a photo of several Native Americans caught her eye. She opened to the Leisure section and skimmed through the lead article. The annual Arizona Native American festival was starting in two days in the small town of Cornville, near Sedona. The article described the event in detail, from the authentic American Indian art and cultural entertainment to the lectures and courses offered.

Alex pulled out her map and glanced at it. Delighted that Cornville was only a state away, she packed her bike and headed west on route 70, visions of red rocks and the desert dancing in her head.

Writer. Author. Inner Activist.

Diane Hatz worked at major and indie record companies, managed a band, and freelanced as a music publicist. She is co-founder of The Relay, a fanzine on The Who, which is in the Rock and Roll Hall of Fame. She's attended thousands of concerts.

During her sometimes-surreal career, Diane founded the nonprofit Change Food, worked to shut down factory farms, organized & spoke at major TED/TEDx events, and executive produced The Meatrix, a Webby Award winner. She has studied with The Dalai Lama and other spiritual teachers.

Diane has an Individualized Master of Arts in Creative Writing from Antioch University in London, England, and is currently focused on writing fiction.

In late 2020, after 30 years living in downtown Manhattan and the East Village, Diane moved to Santa Fe, New Mexico. When not at her computer creating, you can find her hiking, road tripping, or gazing at the stars. The real ones.

www.dianehatz.com &
www.rockgodsandmessymonsters.com

Discussion Questions

- What do you think the book is about? What are the key themes?
- What did you like or dislike?
- How did the book affect you or make you feel?
- What would make someone stay at a job or in a relationship where they're being treated the way Alex is?
- Do you believe entry-level and mid-level staff are still treated this way, even after the #MeToo movement?
- What would you have done if you were Alex?
- What do you think about the main characters?
- Why can it be so hard to break free of situations that aren't good for us?
- What does the receptionist Hellie represent in the book?
- Which scene or scenes stuck out to you and why?
- Do you identify with any of the characters? Why or why not?
- Can you share any experiences you or someone you know has had working in a surreal or trying environment?
- What do you think about the stylistic choice to create a fast-paced fantastical story with a more serious underlying theme?
- Do you have a new perspective as a result of reading this book?
- Did you learn something you didn't know before?

You can find more information at

www.rockgodsandmessymonsters.com

Join Us

If you enjoyed what you read, please join us.

Snap a photo of yourself (or your pet, or…) with the book.
Be creative!

Share your rock god or messy monster story and
post on your favorite social media account(s).

Use **#rockgod** or **#messymonster** and

tag **@wholehealthygroup** and **#rockgodsandmessymonsters**
(@dianehatz on Twitter)

You can also email a copy to
Rock.Gods@yahoo.com

I look forward to reading about your rock god or messy monster
adventures!

Please support the following groups!

Youthworks - www.santafeyouthworks.org

Reconnects at-risk and disadvantaged youth in New Mexico with their community through education, employment training, and job placement.

SocialTees NYC - www.socialteesnyc.org

A foster-based, no-kill rescue in NYC finding forever homes for abandoned dogs and cats.

Green Bronx Machine - www.greenbronxmachine.org

Builds healthy, equitable, and resilient communities through inspired education, local food systems, and 21st Century workforce development.

Harlem Grown - www.harlemgrown.org

To inspire youth to lead healthy and ambitious lives through mentorship and hands-on education in urban farming, sustainability, and nutrition.

Endnote

Thank you for reading *Rock Gods & Messy Monsters*. If you like what you read, please leave a review on any digital platform that sells books (Amazon, Goodreads, Barnes & Noble, Bookshop.org, etc.)
It's much appreciated!

As of June 2022, I'm over 50,000 words into my next novel - an entertaining and fantastical adventure of transformation and redemption. Publication date is not set yet, so please follow me for up-to-date news and info.

Stay in Touch

Sign up for my newsletter "**Next Draft with Diane Hatz**" for an explanation of each chapter of the book, including the meaning and symbolism found throughout. And much more!
dianehatz.substack.com

Email list: wholehealthygroup.com/signup/

Facebook: @dianehatz.author
Instagram & LinkedIn: @wholehealthygroup
Twitter: @dianehatz
Pinterest: @dianemhatz
TikTok: @dianehatz.rockgods
YouTube: bit.ly/YT-RGMM
Ko-fi: @dianehatz

www.rockgodsandmessymonsters.com

Made in the USA
Coppell, TX
06 January 2023

10518481R00125